POWER VOCABULARY

3

BASIC WORD STRATEGIES FOR ADULTS

DOROTHY RUBIN
Trenton State College

CAMBRIDGE Adult Education
REGENTS/PRENTICE HALL
Englewood Cliffs, New Jersey 07632

Library of Congress Cataloging-in-Publication Data

Rubin, Dorothy.
    Power vocabulary : basic word strategies for adults / Dorothy
Rubin.
    "Cambridge adult education".
    ISBN 0-13-678244-2 (v. 1)
    ISBN 0-13-678251-5 (v. 2)
    ISBN 0-13-681198-1 (v. 3)
    1. Vocabulary. 2. English language—Textbooks for foreign
speakers. I. Title.
PE1449.R82 1992
428.1—dc20   91–47734
                          CIP

Acquisitions editor: *Jim Brown*
Editorial/production supervision and interior design: *Louise B. Capuano*
Photo research: *Ellen Diamond*
Cover design: *Carol Ceraldi*
Pre-press buyer: *Ray Keating*
Manufacturing buyer: *Lori Bulwin*
Scheduler: *Leslie Coward*

PHOTO CREDITS
Unit One: Laima Druskis
Unit Two: Irene Springer
Unit Three: Richard Rodaman

 © 1992 by REGENTS/PRENTICE-HALL
A Division of Simon & Schuster
Englewood Cliffs, New Jersey 07632

Printed in the United States of America

10 9 8 7 6 5 4 3 2 1

ISBN 0-13-681198-1

Prentice-Hall International (UK) Limited, *London*
Prentice-Hall of Australia Pty. Limited, *Sydney*
Prentice-Hall Canada Inc., *Toronto*
Prentice-Hall Hispanoamericana, S.A., *Mexico*
Prentice-Hall of India Private Limited, *New Delhi*
Prentice-Hall of Japan, Inc., *Tokyo*
Simon & Schuster Asia Pte. Ltd., *Singapore*
Editora Prentice-Hall do Brasil, Ltda., *Rio de Janeiro*

CONTENTS

Power Vocabulary: Basic Word Strategies for Adults is a five-book series dedicated to helping adults at the ABE level to acquire a basic vocabulary and to gain skill in figuring out word meanings using context clues. *Power Vocabulary* consists of the locator test for the series and five text/workbooks.

There are three units in each of the text/workbooks. The five lessons in each unit present a number of vocabulary words and a variety of context clue strategies. At the end of every unit, there is an **Extra Word Power** section that presents commonly used word parts that can help students unlock many words. There is also a **Words in Sentences** section so that students can demonstrate in writing their ability to use the presented vocabulary words. The sections on **Word Pairs That Go Together** help students develop their verbal reasoning. In addition, the comprehensive Chapter Reviews and Posttests in each book provide skill reinforcement. To facilitate diagnosis, there are Progress Charts for recording students' Chapter Review and Posttest performance. Answers are in a special section at the end of each book. Each book also has a special Glossary and a pronunciation key inside the front cover.

The vocabulary in *Power Vocabulary* is based on graduated levels of difficulty. Each word is presented with the following information: phonetic (pronunciation) spelling of word; kind of word it is; meaning of the word; use of word in a sentence.

Power Vocabulary begins at a very elementary level. Each lesson is a simple and concise presentation of a context clue strategy, and each lesson contains four parts. Each part consists of a short instructional or explanatory section and a practice section.

In the instructional portion of a lesson, under the heading **Read the following,** students study examples of a specific context clue strategy. Under **Did you notice?** they read short, clear explanations of the vocabulary skills and strategies at hand. The **Did you know?** section provides further explanation of how the context clue helps students gain word meanings. Because a typical lesson reinforces and expands upon vocabulary skills and strategies taught in earlier lessons, a section called **Do you remember?** reviews pertinent generalizations and concepts previously presented. The **Try it out** portion of a lesson provides exercises for applying and practicing the new and reviewed vocabulary skills and strategies.

Power Vocabulary encourages the rapid and enjoyable acquisition of a basic vocabulary and context clue strategies. The program is based on sound learning principles and is devised to keep the student actively engaged throughout. It incorporates the following:

- self-pacing
- graduated levels of difficulty
- distributed practice
- immediate feedback
- overlearning
- teaching of generalizations where applicable
- selections based on adult interests
- vocabulary presented in running text

The principle of overlearning, which fosters enduring retention of information, skills, and strategies, is especially stressed in *Power Vocabulary*. Overlearning occurs when students continue practice even after they think they have learned the information. In every lesson, unit, and book in the *Power Vocabulary* series, through a variety of formats, students practice vocabulary skills and strategies they have learned in previous lessons, units, and books. Also, a word once introduced will usually occur in subsequent lessons, and later lessons build on what has been presented earlier.

The structure of the *Power Vocabulary* series makes it versatile. It can be used in conventional classroom settings, in tutorial situations and clinics, or by students who work independently.

Dorothy Rubin

Read the following:

What is the meaning of <u>considerate</u>?

1. José is a considerate person.
2. However, his brother is very selfish.
3. He will not help anyone.
4. He thinks only of himself.

Did you notice?

All the sentences help you figure out the meaning of <u>considerate</u>.
<u>However</u> tells you an opposite follows.
Therefore, you know that <u>selfish</u> is the opposite of <u>considerate</u>.
Sentences 3 and 4 describe a selfish person.
From the clues, you know a considerate person is not selfish.
A considerate person thinks of others.
Therefore, <u>considerate</u> means "caring, nice, or helpful."

Did you know?

Writers often use more than one kind of sentence clue.

Try it out.

Words from this lesson are in sentences.
There is a line under these words.
Use sentence clues to figure out word meanings.
Write the meaning of each underlined word.

1. Mrs. James's car was damaged in a storm. It cost a lot to <u>repair</u> it. It took a month to fix it.

2. Mrs. James wants to know why prices always increase. Why don't they <u>decrease</u>? She has never seen prices go down.

3. She is a <u>fair</u> person. She never cheats others. However, sometimes she often pays more than she should for things.

_____

4. Some workers don't do a good job. They do <u>sloppy</u> work. They are not careful workers.

_____

5. Mrs. James wants everyone to be <u>considerate</u>. People should not think only of themselves. She wants a nice, gentle world. She wants people to help one another.

_____

STOP CHECK ANSWERS ON PAGE 114.

Here are the words in this lesson.
Learn the meanings of the words.

1. **decrease** (dē · krēs′) (Naming word) A becoming or making less or smaller. (Action word) To become or make less or smaller.
   I don't want you to decrease my pay. I want you to increase it.

2. **considerate** (kun · sid′ uh · rit) (Describing word) Thoughtful of the feelings of others; caring of others; unselfish; helpful; nice; kind.
   Mrs. Smith is a considerate person. She cares about other people's feelings.

3. **fair** (fār) (Describing word) Just; the way it should be; blond; light.
   Marcie is fair. She always does what is right. (just)
   Her hair is fair. (blond)
   She has very fair skin. (light)

4. **repair** (ri · pār′) (Naming word) The act of fixing. (Action word) To fix.
   Please help me repair my broken door.

5. **sloppy** (slop′ ē) (Describing word) Messy; not careful; careless; not neat.
   Why is your room so sloppy? Put everything where it belongs.

Try it out.

Below are meanings for each word in this lesson.
Choose the word from the word list that fits the meaning.

WORD LIST

considerate   decrease   fair   repair   sloppy

1. Messy _____

2. Just _____

3. Make smaller _____

4. Caring of others _____

5. Fix _____

STOP   CHECK ANSWERS ON PAGE 114.

Read the following:

1. Alanda helps people a lot.
2. She is very nice.
3. She never hurts anyone.
4. She is considerate.

1. Alanda helps people a lot.
2. She is very nice.
3. She never hurts anyone.
4. She is cruel.

Did you notice?

The word cruel does not fit in sentence 4.
The word considerate fits in sentence 4.
The other sentences help you figure out what word fits.

Try it out.

Fill in each blank. Choose the **best** word for each blank.

1. I would like to _____ your pay. However, I do not have the

   money. (increase or decrease)

2. The _____ woman held the door open for the man. (cruel or

   considerate)

3. Please help me _____ my car. I need to go to work. (break or

   repair)

4. Your room looks _____. Please put your things away. (neat

   or sloppy)

5. Jerry is _____. He never cheats at anything. (fair or unfair)

STOP CHECK ANSWERS ON PAGE 114.

Words that have opposite meanings are called antonyms.
Antonyms are good word clues.
They can help you figure out word meanings.

Try it out.

Here is a story.
It has missing words.
Here is a word list.
Fill in each blank with a word from the word list.
A word may be used only once.

WORD LIST

considerate   decrease   fair   repairs   sloppy

José has a dream. He dreams of a more _____ and gentle
(1)

world. He does not want people to be unkind to one another. He wants to

_____ unhappiness in the world. He also wants people to be
(2)

_____. He does not want people to be unjust. He wants them to
(3)

do what is right. People should not throw garbage on the streets. They

should not be so _____. They should try to keep the streets neat
(4)

and clean. José tries to help others. He _____ broken things
(5)

people throw away. He then gives these to poor people. José is a good man.

Read the following:

What is the meaning of <u>wicked</u>?

1. It is wicked to hurt animals.
2. It is not good.
3. It is evil.

Did you notice?

All the sentences help you figure out the meaning of <u>wicked</u>.
The first sentence gives you an example of something wicked.
The second sentence gives you a word opposite in meaning.
The last sentence gives a word similar in meaning.
Therefore, <u>wicked</u> means "bad" or "evil."

Do you remember?

Writers often use more than one kind of sentence clue.

Try it out.

Words from this lesson are in sentences.
There is a line under these words.
Use sentence clues to figure out word meanings.
Write the meaning of each underlined word.

1. Fernandez has a dangerous job. He <u>guards</u> a bank. He protects it.

_____

2. Most of his work days are <u>ordinary</u> ones. The usual things take place.
   However, one rainy day something unusual took place.

_____

3. It was raining a lot. Everything was very <u>damp</u>. A man came into the
   bank. He was not wet at all. He had a large umbrella with him.

_____

GO ON TO THE NEXT PAGE.

4. Fernandez watched the man. He felt the man was going to do something <u>wicked</u>. He was sure the man was going to do something bad.

---

5. Fernandez saw something <u>glossy</u> inside the umbrella. The man was hiding something shiny in there. Fernandez saw that it was a gun. He quickly walked to the man. Before the man could do anything, Fernandez took away his umbrella and gun. He then called the police.

STOP CHECK ANSWERS ON PAGE 114.

Here are the words in this lesson.
Learn the meanings of the words.

1. **damp** (damp) (Describing word) Wet; moist.
   How could my hair be <u>damp</u>? I washed it four hours ago. It should be dry by now.
2. **glossy** (glos′ ē) (Describing word) Shiny.
   I like my hair to look <u>glossy</u> after I wash it.
3. **guard** (gard) (Naming word) A person who protects someone or something; a person who watches over something or someone.
   (Action word) To protect; to watch over.
   My brother is a <u>guard</u> at a large bank. It is his job to protect the bank.
4. **ordinary** (or′ di · ner · ē) (Describing word) Normal; usual; what you expect.
   This is an <u>ordinary</u> day for her. She is doing all the usual things.
5. **wicked** (wik′ id) (Describing word) Bad; evil.
   The <u>wicked</u> man should be in jail. He is a bad person. He has hurt many people.

Try it out.

Below are meanings for each word in this lesson.
Choose the word from the word list that fits the meaning.

WORD LIST

damp   glossy   guard   ordinary   wicked

1. Bad _____

2. To protect _____

3. Usual _____

4. Shiny _____

5. Moist _____

STOP CHECK ANSWERS ON PAGE 114.

Read the following:

1. It rained all day.	1. It rained all day.
2. I didn't have an umbrella.	2. I didn't have an umbrella.
3. I was in the rain.	3. I was in the rain.
4. My clothes are damp.	4. My clothes are dry.

Did you notice?

The word <u>dry</u> does not fit in sentence 4.
The word <u>damp</u> fits in sentence 4.
The other sentences help you figure out what word fits.

Try it out.

Fill in each blank. Choose the **best** word for each blank.

1. Melissa has done a lot of different things today. She has done things she never did before. She went for an airplane ride. This has not been a(n) _____ day for her. (ordinary or happy)

2. The police said they would _____ the man. Someone was trying to kill him. (ask or guard)

3. It is _____ to hurt people. (fun or wicked)

4. My hair is still _____. I cannot go outside yet. (dry or damp)

5. I polished my car yesterday. It is nice and _____. (sloppy or glossy)

STOP CHECK ANSWERS ON PAGE 114.

SENTENCE CLUES: WORDS WITH THE SAME MEANING (SYNONYMS)

> Words with the same meaning are called synonyms.
> Synonyms are good word clues.
> They can help you figure out word meanings.

Try it out.

Here is a story.
It has missing words.
Here is a word list.
Fill in each blank with a word from the word list.
A word may be used only once.

WORD LIST

damp   glossy   guard   ordinary   wicked

Abdul bought a used car. It was a(n) _____ car. It wasn't
                                       (1)

anything unusual. However, Abdul had never owned a car before. He

worked all day cleaning it. He polished it until it was very shiny. He

wanted it to look nice and _____. He worked hard all
                              (2)

day. Sometimes, some people do _____ things where he lives.
                                    (3)

They damage cars. Therefore, he told the children to watch his car. He told

them he would pay them to _____ it. He left the car windows
                              (4)

open a little. It was very hot out. Just then it started to rain very hard.

He ran to close the car windows. However, the seats of the car did get

_____.
   (5)

STOP CHECK ANSWERS ON PAGE 114.

Read the following:
What is the meaning of <u>gigantic</u>?

1. The Empire State Building is gigantic.
2. This building is gigantic, also.
3. They are both very large.

Did you notice?
Sentences 1 and 2 give you examples of <u>gigantic</u>.
Sentence 3 describes the buildings.
The buildings are both very large.
Therefore, you know that <u>gigantic</u> means "very large."

Did you know?
An example does not give you the meaning of a word.
It gives you clues to the meaning.
An example is one thing that stands for others.

Do you remember?
Writers often use more than one kind of sentence clue.

Try it out.
Words from this lesson are in sentences.
There is a line under these words.
Use sentence clues to figure out word meanings.
Write the meaning of each underlined word.

1. We live on a farm. Our friends live far away. However, we do <u>visit</u> each other a lot. Our friends come to see us one week. We go to see them another week.

---

2. Last year we went to a large city. Every building was <u>gigantic</u>. Each one was bigger than the next. They were all very large.

GO ON TO THE NEXT PAGE.

3. We made plans every day. One day we decided to go to the zoo. Another day we <u>intended</u> to look at the shops. Another day, we wanted to walk around the city.

---

4. We enjoyed walking around the city. However, we saw many people living in the streets. It made us sad to see them. We <u>pitied</u> them. We gave them money. We felt sorry for them.

---

5. It made us feel <u>grateful</u> for what we have. We are thankful for our farm. We feel fortunate that we have a home.

STOP CHECK ANSWERS ON PAGE 114.

Here are the words in this lesson.
Learn the meanings of the words.

1. **gigantic** (jī · gan′ tik) (Describing word) Very large.
   The building is <u>gigantic</u>. It looks as if it is touching the sky.

2. **grateful** (grāt′ ful) (Describing word) Thankful.
   We are <u>grateful</u> for all the things we have.

3. **intend** (in · tend′) (Action word) To plan on doing something; to expect to do something.
   We <u>intend</u> to take a vacation. We plan to go away for the whole summer.

4. **pity** (pi′ tē) (Naming word) A feeling sorry for. (Action word) To feel sorry for.
   We feel <u>pity</u> for all the homeless people.

5. **visit** (viz′ it) (Naming word) A short stay; a coming to see someone or something. (Action word) To go to see someone or something.
   Every Sunday we <u>visit</u> our parents at their house.

Try it out.

Below are meanings for each word in this lesson.
Choose the word from the word list that fits the meaning.

WORD LIST
gigantic   grateful   intend   pity   visit

1. To feel sorry for _____

2. Very large _____

3. To go to see someone or something _____

4. Thankful _____

5. To plan on doing something _____

STOP CHECK ANSWERS ON PAGE 114.

Read the following:

1. Yesterday we went to my aunt's house.
2. Tomorrow we are going to my cousin's house.
3. We like to visit our relatives.

1. Yesterday we went to my aunt's house.
2. Tomorrow we are going to my cousin's house.
3. We like to obey our relatives.

Did you notice?

The word <u>obey</u> does not fit in sentence 3.
The word <u>visit</u> fits in sentence 3.
The other sentences help you figure out what word fits.

Try it out.

Fill in each blank. Choose the **best** word for each blank.

1. What do you _____ to do tomorrow? (complain or intend)

2. We had great _____ for her. She was hurt badly. (success or pity)

3. Please don't _____ me on Tuesday. I'm busy. (intend or visit)

4. Peter is never _____ for anything. I don't like to do anything for him. (selfish or grateful)

5. That is a _____ animal. He must eat a lot. Can he fit in your house? (grateful or gigantic)

STOP CHECK ANSWERS ON PAGE 114.

An example is one thing that stands for others.
Examples are good word clues.

Try it out.

Here is a story.
It has missing words.
Here is a word list.
Fill in each blank with a word from the word list.
A word may be used only once.

WORD LIST

gigantic   grateful   intend   pity   visit

My cousin is a basketball player. He is very tall. Some people say he is

_____ . He has to bend down to go through some doors. I like to
       (1)

_____ him. He always gets me tickets for his games. I
       (2)

_____ to go to a game next week. I am very _____ to
       (3)   (4)

him for getting me tickets. They are hard to get. I enjoy watching him play.

I _____ anyone who has to play against him. My cousin is hard
       (5)

to beat.

STOP CHECK ANSWERS ON PAGE 115.

Read the following:

What is the meaning of <u>bashful</u>?

1. Mary is very bashful.
2. She is afraid to talk to anyone.
3. She is very quiet.
4. She is shy.

Did you notice?

Sentences 2 through 4 help you figure out the meaning of <u>bashful</u>.
Sentences 2 and 3 describe <u>bashful</u>.
Sentence 4 gives you a word with the same meaning.
Therefore, <u>bashful</u> means "shy."

Did you know?

Pictures in words are descriptions.
Descriptions do not give word meanings.
They are clues to word meanings.

Do you remember?

Writers often use more than one kind of sentence clue.

Try it out.

Words from this lesson are in sentences.
There is a line under these words.
Use sentence clues to figure out word meanings.
Write the meaning of each underlined word.

1. Erik's girlfriend loves to dance. Erik, however, does not like to dance.

   He feels <u>awkward</u> when he is dancing. He always steps on his

   girlfriend's toes.

GO ON TO THE NEXT PAGE.

2. Erik <u>refuses</u> to take dancing lessons. He says that he does not want to learn how to dance well.

---

3. His girlfriend thinks he may be <u>bashful</u>. He may be afraid to ask for help.

---

4. His girlfriend loves him. However, she feels it is unusual he does not know how to dance. Erik, however, does not think it is <u>strange</u>.

---

5. Therefore, she is very patient. She wants him to be <u>comfortable</u>. She wants him to feel good when he is with her. She doesn't want him to be miserable.

STOP CHECK ANSWERS ON PAGE 115.

Here are the words in this lesson.
Learn the meanings of the words.

1. **awkward** (awk′wurd) (Describing word) Clumsy; not doing things smoothly; not handy.
   Don't let Tom fix anything. He is very awkward with tools. Last night he banged his hand with the hammer.

2. **bashful** (bash′ ful) (Describing word) Shy; timid.
   Yono doesn't like parties. She is very bashful. She has difficulty talking to people.

3. **comfortable** (kumf′ tuh · bul) (Describing word) Restful; cozy; free from worry.
   I feel comfortable with you. I can be myself. (free from worry)
   This is a very comfortable chair. (cozy; restful)

4. **refuse** (ruh · fūz′) (Action word) To say or show that one is unwilling to accept or do somthing.
   Julio will ask you to the dance. Will you refuse to go with him?

5. **strange** (strānj) (Describing word) Not normal; unusual; not right; new.
   That was a strange thing to do. It is not something she would usually do.

Try it out.

Below are meanings for each word in this lesson.
Choose the word from the word list that fits the meaning.

WORD LIST

awkward   bashful   comfortable   refuse   strange

1. Unusual _____

2. Shy _____

3. To say one is unwilling _____

4. Not doing things smoothly _____

5. Cozy _____

STOP CHECK ANSWERS ON PAGE 115.

Read the following:

1. Larry always drops the ball.
2. He always misses the basket.
3. He falls when he runs.
4. Larry is a very good basketball player.

1. Larry always drops the ball.
2. He always misses the basket.
3. He falls when he runs.
4. Larry is a very awkward basketball player.

Did you notice?

The word <u>good</u> does not fit in sentence 4.
The word <u>awkward</u> fits in sentence 4.
The other sentences help you figure out what word fits.

Try it out.

Fill in each blank. Choose the **best** word for each blank.

1. José loves to meet people. He is always going to parties. He is very

   _____ . (friendly or bashful)

2. His sister does not like anything unusual. She likes to go to the same

   places. She does not like _____ places. (patient or strange)

3. I like to stay at home. I enjoy reading in my _____ chair.

   (awkward or comfortable)

4. I had to take the job. They were giving me everything I wanted. I could

   not _____ . (refuse or pity)

5. The hem she sewed is crooked. She is very _____ with a

   needle and thread. (comfortable or awkward)

STOP CHECK ANSWERS ON PAGE 115.

A picture in words helps you figure out word meanings.
It is a good word clue.

Try it out.

Here is a story.
It has missing words.
Here is a word list.
Fill in each blank with a word from the word list.
A word may be used only once.

WORD LIST

awkward   bashful   comfortable   refuse   strange

Taking care of children is not easy. Young children are often

_____ with their hands. When children spill things, parents
(1)

should not yell. Good parents need to be patient. They need to know when

to say "yes." They need to know when to _____ to do some things.
(2)

Good parents give their children lots of love. Their children feel safe. They

feel _____ at home. Good parents help children to be friendly and
(3)

outgoing. They do not want their children to be _____. They
(4)

want them to like people. They want people to like them. However, good

parents tell their children to be careful. They tell their children not to talk

to _____ people.
(5)

STOP CHECK ANSWERS ON PAGE 115.

Read the following:

What is the meaning of <u>advertisement</u>?

1. Hassid put an advertisement in the newspaper.
2. He wants to sell his car.
3. People will read the newspaper.
4. Some people may call Hassid about his car.
5. Then someone may buy it.

Did you notice?

All the sentences give you clues to the meaning of <u>advertisement</u>. They give you reasons why Hassid put the advertisement in the newspaper.

An advertisement tells about something for sale in a newspaper, on the radio, or on television.

Did you know?

Knowing the reason for something can help you figure out word meanings.

Try it out.

Words from this lesson are in sentences.
There is a line under these words.
Use sentence clues to figure out word meanings.
Write the meaning of each underlined word.

1. Maria was going to school. However, she also needed to work. She wanted a <u>part-time</u> job. She could work mornings. Then she could go to school afternoons.

GO ON TO THE NEXT PAGE.

2. She looked at the job <u>advertisements</u> in the newspaper. Many jobs were listed there.

---

3. She saw an interesting job listed. It was for a <u>secretary</u>. The person needed someone to type letters. The person needed someone to answer the phone and file papers.

---

4. Maria called the person. He invited her to meet with him. Maria <u>rushed</u> to his office. She wanted to get there before anyone else.

---

5. Maria was <u>hopeful</u>. The man sounded nice on the phone. Also, he seemed to like her. However, at the office there were already four people waiting. They were all there for the same job. Maria waited to meet the man. It's fortunate she did. She got the job.

STOP CHECK ANSWERS ON PAGE 115.

Here are the words in this lesson.
Learn the meanings of the words.

1. **advertisement** (ad · vur · tīz′ mint) or (ad · vur′ tiz · mint) (Naming word)   A notice of things for sale in a newspaper, on the radio, or on television; a list of jobs in a newspaper.
We looked at the advertisements for used cars in the newspaper.

2. **hopeful** (hōp′ ful) (Describing word)   Feeling that what you want to take place will take place; expecting to get what you want.
We are hopeful that we will find a used car we like.

3. **part-time** (part′ - tīm′) (Describing word)   Working fewer hours than usual; working less than a full day; not working a full day.
I am going to school. Therefore, I want a part-time job.

4. **rush** (rush) (Naming word)   The act of moving quickly or fast; the act of hurrying.   (Action word)   To move quickly; to move fast; to hurry.
Andy fell off a ladder. We rushed him to the hospital.

5. **secretary** (sek′ ruh · ter · ē) (Describing word)   An office worker who answers the phone and letters for a boss.
My brother works in an office. His secretary answers all his letters.

Try it out.

Below are meanings for each word in this lesson.
Choose the word from the word list that fits the meaning.

WORD LIST

advertisement   hopeful   part-time   rush   secretary

1. Working fewer hours than usual _____

2. An office worker who answers the phone and letters for a boss

_____

GO ON TO THE NEXT PAGE.

3. Expecting to get what you want _____

4. A job listed in a newspaper _____

5. To move quickly _____

STOP CHECK ANSWERS ON PAGE 115.

SENTENCE CLUES: THE REASON FOR SOMETHING (EXPLANATION)

5

Read the following:

1. Don wanted to sell his car.
2. Therefore, he put an advertisement in the newspaper.

1. Don wanted to sell his car.
2. Therefore, he put a secretary in the newspaper.

Did you notice?

The word <u>secretary</u> does not fit in sentence 2.
The word <u>advertisement</u> fits in sentence 2.
The other sentence helps you figure out what word fits.

Try it out.

Fill in each blank. Choose the **best** word for each blank.

1. My cousin is very ill. We are _____ that she will be better soon. (fair or hopeful)

2. My sister has a _____ job only. She doesn't have the time to work more hours. (hopeful or part-time)

3. Did the _____ help you get a job? Which paper was it in? (secretary or advertisement)

4. We need to catch an early bus. We need to _____ to make it. (visit or rush)

5. I am a good _____ . I enjoy opening the mail. I like to write letters. (parent or secretary)

STOP CHECK ANSWERS ON PAGE 115.

26

> The reason for something is called an explanation.
> Explanations are good sentence clues.
> They can help you figure out word meanings.

Try it out.

Here is a story.
It has missing words.
Here is a word list.
Fill in each blank with a word from the word list.
A word may be used only once.

WORD LIST

advertisement   hopeful   part-time   rush   secretary

Mary Brown is a(n) _____ . She works in a large office.
(1)

Her job is to type letters and open the mail. She got her job from a(n)

_____ in the newspaper. Everyone said she would not get the job.
(2)

However, Mary was _____ that she would get it. She was very
(3)

grateful to the boss for giving it to her. It is a good job because it's a

_____ job. She only works from 9:00 A.M. to 2:00 P.M. Then she
(4)

can _____ home. She likes to be home when her children come
(5)

home from school.

STOP   CHECK ANSWERS ON PAGE 115.

EXTRA WORD POWER

Ly. In what way (how something is done).

Ly is found at the end of many words. **Ly** at the end of a word usually means "in what way" (how something is done).

Examples with ly: slowly—in a slow way; quickly—in a quick way; happily—in a happy way; sadly—in a sad way; sloppily—in a sloppy way; nicely—in a nice way; noisily—in a noisy way; busily—in a busy way.

How many more **ly** words can you think of?

Special Note: For words that end in **y**, we usually change the **y** to **i** before adding the ending **ly.** Examples: happy → happily; sloppy → sloppily; noisy → noisily; busy → busily.

WORDS IN SENTENCES (LESSONS 1–5)

Here are sentences using some of the words in this unit.
Examples:

1. (awkward; sloppy)
   That person is awkward and sloppy.
2. (advertisement; part-time)
   Here is an advertisement for a part-time job.

Try it out.

Write a sentence with the words given below.

1. (considerate; visit)

_____

2. (guard; refuse)

_____

3. (awkward; pity)

_____

4. (secretary; sloppy)

_____

5. (grateful; repair)

_____

STOP CHECK SAMPLE SENTENCES ON PAGE 115.

WORD PAIRS THAT GO TOGETHER (ANALOGIES)

Read the following:

1. <u>Fast</u> is to <u>slow</u> as <u>late</u> is to <u>early</u>.   (opposites)
2. <u>Clever</u> is to <u>smart</u> as <u>damp</u> is to <u>wet</u>.   (same meanings)
3. <u>Fall</u> is to <u>season</u> as <u>California</u> is to <u>state</u>.   (examples)

Did you notice?

The first and second sets in each sentence have the same kinds of pairs.

Did you know?

Two sets put together must have the same kinds of pairs.

Try it out.

Here is a word list.
Choose the word that **best** fits the blank.
A word may be used only once.

WORD LIST

gigantic   increase   just   restful   usual

1. Repair is to fix as ordinary is to _____.

2. Considerate is to selfish as decrease is to _____.

3. Damp is to wet as comfortable is to _____.

4. Frequently is to often as fair is to _____.

5. Baby is to small as Empire State Building is to _____.

STOP   CHECK ANSWERS ON PAGE 115.

WORD PAIRS THAT GO TOGETHER (ANALOGIES)

Read the following:

1. <u>Divorce</u> is to <u>marry</u> as <u>damp</u> is to <u>dry</u>. (opposites)
2. <u>Glad</u> is to <u>happy</u> as <u>bashful</u> is to <u>shy</u>. (same meanings)
3. <u>Dime</u> is to <u>money</u> as <u>chicken</u> is to <u>fowl</u>. (examples)

Did you notice?

The first and second sets in each sentence have the same kinds of pairs.

Do you remember?

Two sets put together must have the same kinds of pairs.

Try it out.

Here is a word list.
Choose the word that **best** fits the blank.
Not all the words fit.
A word may be used only once.

WORD LIST

awkward   best   boss   careful   guard   outgoing
thankful   timid   ungrateful   wicked

1. Annoy is to bother as bashful is to _____.

2. Price is to cost as grateful is to _____.

3. Miserable is to happy as good is to _____.

4. Rush is to hurry as protect is to _____.

5. Expensive is to costly as clumsy is to _____.

STOP CHECK ANSWERS ON PAGE 115.

LESSON 1

Match each word with its meaning.

____	1. decrease	**a.**	fix
____	2. fair	**b.**	messy
____	3. considerate	**c.**	to make smaller
____	4. repair	**d.**	caring of others
____	5. sloppy	**e.**	just

LESSON 2

Match each word with its meaning.

____	1. damp	**a.**	usual
____	2. glossy	**b.**	to protect
____	3. guard	**c.**	evil
____	4. ordinary	**d.**	shiny
____	5. wicked	**e.**	moist

LESSON 3

Match each word with its meaning.

____	1. gigantic	**a.**	thankful
____	2. grateful	**b.**	to go to see someone
____	3. pity	**c.**	to plan on doing something
____	4. intend	**d.**	very large
____	5. visit	**e.**	to feel sorry for

GO ON TO THE NEXT PAGE.

LESSON 4

Match each word with its meaning.

___ 1. bashful   a. unusual

___ 2. awkward   b. shy

___ 3. comfortable   c. to say one is unwilling to accept

___ 4. strange   d. cozy

___ 5. refuse   e. clumsy

LESSON 5

Match each word with its meaning.

___ 1. advertisement   a. working fewer hours than usual

___ 2. hopeful   b. an office worker who answers the phone and letters for a boss

___ 3. part-time   c. a list of things for sale in a newspaper or on radio or TV

___ 4. rush   d. expecting to get what you want

___ 5. secretary   e. to move fast

STOP CHECK ANSWERS ON PAGE 116.

Count how many items you answered correctly in each review lesson. Write your score for each review lesson in the My Scores column. If all your scores are as high as the Good Scores, go on to Unit Two. If any of your review lesson scores are lower than the Good Scores, study the Review Pages. Then go on to Unit Two.

Lesson	Good Scores	My Scores	Review Pages
1	4 or 5		2–6
2	4 or 5		7–11
3	4 or 5		12–16
4	4 or 5		17–21
5	4 or 5		22–27

Read the following:

What is the meaning of <u>excited</u>?

1. Abdul was very excited.
2. He couldn't sit still.
3. He won a new car.
4. No one in his family was calm.

Did you notice?

Sentences 2 through 4 help you figure out the meaning of <u>excited</u>.
Sentence 2 describes the word.
Sentence 3 tells you why Abdul is excited.
Sentence 4 gives you a word opposite in meaning to excited.
Therefore, <u>excited</u> means "not calm."
It means "showing strong feeling."

Do you remember?

Writers often use more than one kind of sentence clue.

Try it out.

Words from this lesson are in sentences.
There is a line under these words.
Use sentence clues to figure out word meanings.
Write the meaning of each underlined word.

1. Abdul almost fainted. He couldn't believe he had won a car. He had

   never won anything so <u>valuable</u>. He had never won anything worth so

   much.

2. Abdul phoned his wife. She was very <u>excited</u>. Abdul told her to remain

   calm. She said she couldn't.

GO ON TO THE NEXT PAGE.

3. She said she felt like shouting the news to everyone. Abdul said she shouldn't even <u>whisper</u> it. He wanted to keep it quiet.

---

4. Abdul said he would receive the car in a week. However, he wasn't <u>positive</u> about the date. He was unsure about that. However, he was sure that the car was his.

---

5. Abdul said that they should <u>conceal</u> the news. They should not tell anyone else about it. It would be a secret.

STOP CHECK ANSWERS ON PAGE 116.

WORDS AND THEIR MEANINGS

Here are the words in this lesson.
Learn the meanings of the words.

1. **conceal** (kun · sēl′) (Action word)   To hide; to keep secret; to place out of sight.
They wanted to conceal the news. They wanted to keep it secret.
2. **excited** (ek · sīt′ id) (Describing word)   Having or showing strong feelings; stirred up by feeling.
The excited man started to yell loudly.
3. **positive** (poz′ uh · tiv) (Describing word)   Sure; certain.
I am positive she and Mike are married.
4. **valuable** (val′ ū · uh · bul) (Describing word)   Costing a lot of money; worth a lot.
I have a valuable ring. It cost a lot of money.
5. **whisper** (whis′ per) (Naming word)   Talking that is very soft.
(Action word)   To talk very softly.
The baby is asleep. Please whisper. Do not wake her up.

Try it out.

Below are meanings for each word in this lesson.
Choose the word from the word list that fits the meaning.

WORD LIST
conceal   excited   positive   valuable   whisper

1. To keep secret _____

2. To speak softly _____

3. Having or showing strong feelings _____

4. Worth a lot _____

5. Certain _____

STOP   CHECK ANSWERS ON PAGE 116.

38

SENTENCE CLUES: OPPOSITES (ANTONYMS) 6

Read the following:

1. Lin's wife just had a baby.
2. He rushed to phone everyone.
3. He couldn't sit still.
4. Lin was very excited.

1. Lin's wife just had a baby.
2. He rushed to phone everyone.
3. He couldn't sit still.
4. Lin was very calm.

Did you notice?

The word calm does not fit in sentence 4.

The word excited fits in sentence 4.

The other sentences help you figure out what word fits.

Try it out.

Fill in each blank. Choose the **best** word for each blank.

1. Fred guards _____ things. They cost a lot of money. (positive or valuable)

2. Sometimes, he cannot tell anyone what he guards. He has to _____ it. (whisper or conceal)

3. Fred likes his job. He was very _____ about getting it. (bashful or excited)

4. He was _____ he would be a good guard. (worried or positive)

5. He used to work in a library. There everyone spoke in a _____. It was hard for him. He has a loud voice. (dream or whisper)

CHECK ANSWERS ON PAGE 116.

39

SENTENCE CLUES: OPPOSITES (ANTONYMS) 6

Words that have opposite meanings are called antonyms.
Antonyms are good word clues.
They can help you figure out word meanings.

Try it out.

Here is a story.
It has missing words.
Here is a word list.
Fill in each blank with a word from the word list.
A word may be used only once.

WORD LIST

conceal   excited   positive   valuable   whisper

Kim Jones knew something. Kim Jones had to _____ it. She
(1)

didn't want anyone to know about it. Kim couldn't read or write. She was

afraid someone would find this out. She didn't want people to

_____ about her. She didn't want people talking about her behind
(2)

her back. There was only one thing to do. She had to learn to read and

write. So she went back to school. She was very _____ about it.
(3)

She couldn't wait to begin. It is very _____ to know how to read
(4)

and write. It will be worth a lot to her. She was _____ she could
(5)

learn to read and write. She was right. It wasn't easy, but she did learn.

STOP CHECK ANSWERS ON PAGE 116.

Read the following:

What is the meaning of <u>mild</u>?

1. Is that a mild soap?
2. You can only put gentle things on a baby's skin.
3. You should not use anything harsh.

Did you notice?

Sentences 2 and 3 give you clues to the meaning of <u>mild</u>.
<u>Gentle</u> and <u>mild</u> have the same meaning.
<u>Harsh</u> and <u>mild</u> are opposite in meaning.
Therefore, <u>mild</u> means "gentle."

Do you remember?

Writers often use more than one kind of sentence clue.

Try it out.

Words from this lesson are in sentences.
There is a line under these words.
Use sentence clues to figure out word meanings.
Write the meaning of each underlined word.

1. There was a <u>mild</u> wind today. I liked the gentle breeze. I had nice

   weather for the last day of my vacation.

2. I have lots of <u>additional</u> work to do this week. I always have more work

   after a vacation.

GO ON TO THE NEXT PAGE.

3. I am taking many tests this week. I feel <u>anxious</u> about them. I am really worried. I need to do well.

_____

4. I <u>appreciate</u> what my teachers are doing for me. I value their help. I am grateful for it.

_____

5. However, they cannot <u>guarantee</u> that I will do well. They cannot make such a promise. I have to work hard to do well.

_____

STOP CHECK ANSWERS ON PAGE 116.

Here are the words in this lesson.
Learn the meanings of the words.

1. **additional** (uh · dish′ un · ul) (Describing word)   More; extra.
   I will need to work <u>additional</u> hours next week. If I don't work more, I won't get my work done.

2. **anxious** (ank′ shus) (Describing word)   Worried; uneasy.
   I am <u>anxious</u> about getting work. I can't find a job.

3. **appreciate** (uh · prē′ shē · āt) (Action word)   To feel grateful; to value; to be thankful.
   I <u>appreciate</u> what you did. You helped me get a job.

4. **guarantee** (gar · un · tē′) (Naming word)   A promise; an agreement that something will be done or will work. (Action word)   To promise; to promise that something will be done or will work.
   I <u>guarantee</u> that I will finish the work on time.

5. **mild** (mīld) (Describing word)   Gentle; soft; not harsh; not strong.
   I have a <u>mild</u> cold.   (not strong)
   The breeze is <u>mild</u>.   (gentle)
   This is a <u>mild</u> winter.   (not harsh)

Try it out.

Below are meanings for each word in this lesson.
Choose the word from the word list that fits the meaning.

WORD LIST
         additional   anxious   appreciate   guarantee   mild

1. Gentle _____

2. A promise _____

3. To value _____

4. More _____

5. Worried _____

STOP   CHECK ANSWERS ON PAGE 116.

43

Read the following:

1. Maria's mother is ill.
2. Maria is worried about her.
3. She is happy about her mother's illness.

1. Maria's mother is ill.
2. Maria is worried about her.
3. She is anxious about her mother's illness.

Did you notice?

The word <u>happy</u> does not fit in sentence 3.
The word <u>anxious</u> fits in sentence 3.
The other sentences help you figure out what word fits.

Try it out.

Fill in each blank. Choose the **best** word for each blank.

1. Hannah does not _____ anything we do. She never says, "Thank you." She thinks everything is coming to her. (appreciate or guarantee)

2. Hannah never does any _____ work for anyone. (mild or additional)

3. She _____ that she will do things. However, she never does them. You can't believe her promises. (guarantees or appreciates)

4. She may lose her job. However, she is not _____ about it. Nothing worries her. (mild or anxious)

5. However, she gets angry if she gets a _____ cold. (damp or mild)

STOP CHECK ANSWERS ON PAGE 116.

Words with the same meaning are called synonyms.
Synonyms are good word clues.
They can help you figure out word meanings.

Try it out.

Here is a story.
It has missing words.
Here is a word list.
Fill in each blank with a word from the word list.
A word may be used only once.

WORD LIST

additional   anxious   appreciate   guarantee   mild

Anton's mother is elderly. Anton is very _____ about her. He
(1)

is worried about her living alone. His mother does not want extra help from

anyone. However, Anton feels she needs _____ care. She has had
(2)

a(n) _____ heart attack. It was not serious. However, Anton
(3)

wants someone to live with her and help her. His mother is a very proud

woman. She wants to live alone. She does not _____ what her
(4)

son wants to do. She does not thank him. Anton spoke to his mother. He

said the doctor could not _____ her good health. If she does not
(5)

get help, the doctor cannot promise that she will be all right.

STOP CHECK ANSWERS ON PAGE 117.

45

Read the following:

What is the meaning of <u>advice</u>?

1. Vera needs help.
2. She doesn't know what to do.
3. Everyone is giving her advice.
4. Fred is telling her to go home.
5. Sue is telling her not to go home.

Did you notice?

All the sentences give you clues to the meaning of <u>advice</u>.
Sentences 4 and 5 are examples of advice.
They help you figure out the meaning of <u>advice</u>.
<u>Advice</u> means "what someone says you should do."

Do you remember?

Examples do not give you the meaning of a word.
An example is one thing that stands for others.
Examples help you figure out word meanings.

Try it out.

Words from this lesson are in sentences.
There is a line under these words.
Use sentence clues to figure out word meanings.
Write the meaning of each underlined word.

1. Marie owns a <u>bakery</u>. She sells all kinds of cookies, cakes, and bread.

---

2. She is hard-working. Her hard work has helped her earn a <u>fortune</u>. She

   now has lots of money.

GO ON TO THE NEXT PAGE.

3. Marie makes the cookies herself. She makes a <u>variety</u> of cookies. She makes all different kinds. For example, she makes nut cookies, raisin cookies, and chocolate cookies.

---

4. Marie always invited people to her home. She would give her <u>guests</u> the cookies she made. They loved the cookies.

---

5. People said, "Marie, you should go into the cookie business." She took their <u>advice</u>.

STOP CHECK ANSWERS ON PAGE 117.

Here are the words in this lesson.
Learn the meanings of the words.

1. **advice** (ad · vīs′) (Naming word) What you tell people you think they should do; what someone says you should do.
   I can't give you any <u>advice</u>. I don't know what you should do.

2. **bakery** (bā′ kuh · rē) (Naming word) A place where bread, cookies, and cakes are made and sold.
   I buy all my bread from that <u>bakery</u>. Their bread is delicious.

3. **fortune** (for′ chun) (Naming word) A lot of money; riches; luck; what will happen to you.
   He won a <u>fortune</u> in the lottery.   (a lot of money)
   It was my <u>fortune</u> to lose the game.   (luck)
   Should I tell you your <u>fortune</u>?   (what will happen to you)

4. **guest** (gest) (Naming word) A person visiting another's home or someplace.
   My parents always have <u>guests</u> at our home during the holidays.

5. **variety** (vuh · rī′ uh · tē) (Naming word) Many different kinds of things.
   We do not like to do the same things every day. We enjoy <u>variety</u>.

Try it out.

Below are meanings for each word in this lesson.
Choose the word from the word list that fits the meaning.

WORD LIST

advice   bakery   fortune   guest   variety

1. Different kinds of things _____

2. A lot of money _____

3. A person visiting someone's home _____

4. A place where bread, cake, and cookies are made and sold

   _____

5. What someone says you should do _____

STOP CHECK ANSWERS ON PAGE 117.

Read the following:

1. Ying doesn't know what to do.
2. He can't make up his mind.
3. He needs good advice.

1. Ying doesn't know what to do.
2. He can't make up his mind.
3. He needs good fortune.

Did you notice?

The word <u>fortune</u> does not fit in sentence 3.
The word <u>advice</u> fits in sentence 3.
The other sentences help you figure out what word fits.

Try it out.

Fill in each blank. Choose the **best** word for each blank.

1. Joe can buy anything he wants. He has a _____. (bakery or fortune)

2. I'm happy I own a _____. I love bread and cake. (fortune or bakery)

3. We are having a _____ for dinner. (guest or fortune)

4. Marcie doesn't like to eat the same foods. She likes a _____ of foods. (fortune or variety)

5. What _____ can you give us? We don't know what to do. (variety or advice)

STOP CHECK ANSWERS ON PAGE 117.

Examples are things that stand for other things.
Examples are good word clues.
They can help you figure out word meanings.

Try it out.

Here is a story.
It has missing words.
Here is a word list.
Fill in each blank with a word from the word list.
A word may be used only once.

WORD LIST

advice   bakery   fortune   guest   variety

Every _____ who comes to Philippe's house loves his bread.
(1)

Each one says, "Philippe, you should open a(n) _____." Philippe
(2)

wants to have his own business. However, he doesn't have the money he

needs. It takes a(n) _____ to start a business. You have to buy
(3)

a(n) _____ of things. He needs to talk to someone who owns a
(4)

business. He needs some good _____ .
(5)

STOP CHECK ANSWERS ON PAGE 117.

Read the following:

What is the meaning of <u>peculiar</u>?

1. I did not feel right.
2. I felt different from my normal self.
3. I felt peculiar.

Did you notice?

Sentences 1 and 2 describe peculiar.
Someone who feels peculiar feels different.
He or she does not feel normal.
Therefore, <u>peculiar</u> means "not normal" or "strange."
It means "unusual."

Do you remember?

Pictures in words are descriptions.
Descriptions do not give word meanings.
They are clues to word meanings.

Try it out.

Words from this lesson are in sentences.
There is a line under these words.
Use sentence clues to figure out word meanings.
Write the meaning of each underlined word.

1. Mary feels it's <u>peculiar</u> that Jim hasn't phoned yet. He always phones

   when he is late. She feels it is strange that he hasn't phoned.

2. Jim is very <u>dependable</u>. If he says he will phone, he phones. You can

   count on him. He always does what he says he will do.

GO ON TO THE NEXT PAGE.

3. Jim is out looking at a new <u>apartment</u>. The apartment is large. It has four rooms, and it's in a nice building. The rooms are sunny.

---

4. The apartment would be <u>perfect</u> for them. It's what they need. It couldn't be any better. The price is right, too.

---

5. Jim wants to <u>surprise</u> Mary. He didn't tell her where he was going. He wanted to see if he could get the apartment first. She doesn't know anything about this.

STOP CHECK ANSWERS ON PAGE 117.

WORDS AND THEIR MEANINGS

Here are the words in this lesson.
Learn the meanings of the words.

1. **apartment** (uh · part′ ment) (Naming word) A room or set of rooms in a building in which people live.
I live in a nice four room <u>apartment</u> in the city.
2. **dependable** (di · pen′ duh · bul) (Describing word) Able to be sure of; able to be counted on; always doing what one should.
My clock is very <u>dependable</u>. It always tells the right time.
3. **peculiar** (pi · kūl′ yur) (Describing word) Not normal; unusual; out of the ordinary; strange; odd.
That was a <u>peculiar</u> thing to do. It's not something I'd expect of you.
4. **perfect** (pur′ fikt) (Describing word) The best something can be; without anything wrong.
This dress is <u>perfect</u>. It couldn't fit me better.
5. **surprise** (sur · prīz′) (Naming word) Something that someone doesn't expect. (Action word) To do something that someone doesn't expect.
We did not expect to see them. Their visit was a <u>surprise</u>.

Try it out.

Below are meanings for each word in this lesson.
Choose the word from the word list that fits the meaning.

WORD LIST

apartment   dependable   peculiar   perfect   surprise

1. Strange _____

2. Something that someone doesn't expect _____

3. Able to be counted on _____

4. A room or set of rooms in a building in which people live

_____

5. The best something can be _____

STOP CHECK ANSWERS ON PAGE 117.

Read the following:

1. This room is perfect for me.
2. I like the colors.
3. The windows are large.
4. The ceiling is high.
5. It's great.

1. This room is wrong for me.
2. I like the colors.
3. The windows are large.
4. The ceiling is high.
5. It's great.

Did you notice?

The word <u>wrong</u> does not fit in sentence 1.
The word <u>perfect</u> fits in sentence 1.
The other sentences help you figure out what word fits.

Try it out.

Fill in each blank. Choose the **best** word for each blank.

1. If Sanchez says he will do something, he does it. He is _____.
   (peculiar or dependable)

2. I like my _____. The rooms are large and sunny. (fortune or apartment)

3. My husband is _____. He is kind and good. He helps me a lot. (sloppy or perfect)

4. Isn't it _____ to wear a winter coat when it's so hot? (peculiar or perfect)

5. My boyfriend gave me a big _____ on my birthday. I didn't expect an expensive ring. (success or surprise)

STOP CHECK ANSWERS ON PAGE 117.

A picture in words describes something.
A picture in words is a good sentence clue.
It can help you figure out word meanings.

Try it out.

Here is a story.
It has missing words.
Here is a word list.
Fill in each blank with a word from the word list.
A word may be used only once.

WORD LIST

apartments   dependable   peculiar   perfect   surprise

A(n) _____ man was in our building. He looked very odd. He
            (1)

frightened the children. We did not let our children leave our

_____. We called the police. They are _____. They
   (2)   (3)

came very quickly. The police took the man away. The man was wanted for

many things. He tells children he has a(n) _____ for them. Many
                                                  (4)

children go with him to find out what it is. Then he hurts them. We know

our children are not _____. However, we try to help them to be
                           (5)

good. We tell them not to go with strangers.

STOP CHECK ANSWERS ON PAGE 117.

Read the following:

What is the meaning of disguise?

1. I am going to a party.
2. I have to come looking like a different person.
3. I will wear a disguise.
4. I will dress as a cowboy.
5. I don't want anyone to know who I am.
6. I will wear a mask, too.

Did you notice?

These sentences give you clues to the meaning of disguise.
They give you reasons why the person will wear a disguise.
They also describe what a disguise is.
A disguise is "the wearing of clothing or a mask to hide who a person is."

Did you know?

Knowing the reason for something can help you figure out word meanings.
The reason for something is called an explanation.

Do you remember?

Writers often use more than one kind of sentence clue.

Try it out.

Words from this lesson are in sentences.
There is a line under these words.
Use sentence clues to figure out word meanings.
Write the meaning of each underlined word.

1. Be careful how you hold the vase. It is very fragile.

GO ON TO THE NEXT PAGE.

2. This vase is very valuable. Once, some of our things were stolen. We never found the <u>thief</u>.

---

3. We were very <u>distressed</u>. It upset us that someone would steal from us.

---

4. This vase is truly <u>extraordinary</u>. It is very unusual. They don't make vases like this anymore.

---

5. We tried to <u>disguise</u> some of our valuable things. We tried to make them look plain and ordinary. However, we didn't fool the robbers.

STOP CHECK ANSWERS ON PAGE 117.

Here are the words in this lesson.
Learn the meanings of the words.

1. **disguise** (dis · gīz′) (Naming word)   Something that makes someone or something look like someone or something else; clothes or mask that hide who a person is.   (Action word)   To hide who one is by wearing certain clothing or a mask; to try to look like someone or something else.
He wore such a good <u>disguise</u>. We couldn't tell who he was.

2. **distress** (dis · tres′) (Naming word)   Pain; upset.   (Action word)   To cause sadness or pain; to upset.
I cannot describe the <u>distress</u> I felt when my dog died.

3. **extraordinary** (ik · strord′ un · er · ē) or (ek · struh · ord′ un · er · ē) (Describing word)   Very unusual; great; going far beyond the ordinary.
Bruce gave an <u>extraordinary</u> talk. He is a very great speaker.

4. **fragile** (fraj′ ul) (Describing word)   Very delicate; easily broken.
Tom was afraid to hold the baby. She looked so <u>fragile</u>.

5. **thief** (thēf) (Naming word)   Robber; crook; a person who steals.
The police caught the <u>thief</u>. He had robbed many stores.

Try it out.

Below are meanings for each word in this lesson.
Choose the word from the word list that fits the meaning.

WORD LIST

disguise   distress   extraordinary   fragile   thief

1. Crook _____

2. Very unusual _____

3. To cause sadness or pain _____

4. Very delicate _____

5. Something that makes someone look like another _____

STOP CHECK ANSWERS ON PAGE 117.

Read the following:

1. The woman stole a dress.
2. She put it under her coat.
3. The guard saw her do it.
4. He said, "Stop."
5. He caught the thief.

1. The woman stole a dress.
2. She put it under her coat.
3. The guard saw her do it.
4. He said, "Stop."
5. He caught the secretary.

Did you notice?

The word <u>secretary</u> does not fit in sentence 5.
The word <u>thief</u> fits in sentence 5.
The other sentences help you figure out what word fits.

Try it out.

Fill in each blank. Choose the **best** word for each blank.

1. He wore a very good _____. He looked just like Superman. (suit or disguise)

2. My mother is very _____. She is very old. If she falls she can easily break her hip. (extraordinary or fragile)

3. The sun is out. Yet it is raining. That is _____ _____. (mild or extraordinary)

4. He is always in _____. He has many problems. (disguise or distress)

5. The man stole the watch. He was sent to jail as a _____. (leader or thief)

A reason for something tells why something is done.
A reason for something is a good sentence clue.
It can help you figure out word meanings.

Try it out.

Here is a story.
It has missing words.
Here is a word list.
Fill in each blank with a word from the word list.
A word may be used only once.

WORD LIST

disguise   distress   extraordinary   fragile   thief

Something _____ took place last week. It was really very
     (1)

unusual. It took place outside my apartment. I heard loud crying. I opened

my door. I saw a tiny baby wrapped in a blanket. It looked so

_____. Someone had left it at my door. It seemed to be in
  (2)

_____. It cried and cried. I called the police. They came right
  (3)

over. They said a woman had taken the baby from the hospital. This

_____ had stolen a nurse's uniform. She wore it as a(n)
   (4)

_____. Dressed as a nurse, she took the baby. The police said she
  (5)

must have gotten frightened. That is why she left the baby outside my

apartment.

STOP   CHECK ANSWERS ON PAGE 118.

EXTRA WORD POWER

Able. Can do; able to.

Able is found at the end of many words. **Able** at the end of a word means "can do"; "able to." **Able** at the end of a word usually makes the word a describing word.

Examples with able: laughable—able to be laughed at; enjoyable—able to be enjoyed; lovable—able to be loved; breakable—able to be broken; likable—able to be liked; dependable—able to be depended on; returnable—able to be returned; movable—able to be moved.

How many more **able** words can you think of?

WORDS IN SENTENCES (LESSONS 6–10)

Here are sentences using some of the words in this unit.
Examples:

1. (excited; guest)
   We are excited you will be our guest.
2. (positive; secret)
   I am positive it is a secret.

Try it out.

Write a sentence with the words given below.

1. (variety; bakery)

_____

2. (perfect; apartment)

_____

3. (excited; surprise)

_____

4. (appreciate; advice)

_____

5. (peculiar; disguise)

_____

STOP   CHECK SAMPLE SENTENCES ON PAGE 118.

WORD PAIRS THAT GO TOGETHER (ANALOGIES)

Read the following:

1. <u>Always</u> is to <u>never</u> as <u>fair</u> is to <u>dark</u>. (opposites)
2. <u>Glossy</u> is to <u>shiny</u> as <u>guard</u> is to <u>protect</u>. (same meanings)
3. <u>Secretary</u> is to <u>job</u> as <u>bakery</u> is to <u>business</u>. (examples)

Did you notice?

The first and second sets in each sentence have the same kinds of pairs.

Do you remember?

Two sets put together must have the same kinds of pairs.

Try it out.

Here is a word list.
Choose the word that **best** fits the blank.
Not all the words fit.
A word may be used only once.

WORD LIST

angry	annoy	apartment	fortune	gentle
harsh	promise	strong	unusual	usual

1. Timid is to bashful as guarantee is to _____.

2. Repair is to fix as mild is to _____.

3. Sloppy is to neat as fragile is to _____.

4. Mask is to disguise as room is to _____.

5. Additional is to more as extraordinary is to _____.

STOP CHECK ANSWERS ON PAGE 118.

WORD PAIRS THAT GO TOGETHER (ANALOGIES)

Read the following:

1. <u>Slender</u> is to <u>fat</u> as <u>positive</u> is to <u>unsure</u>. (opposites)
2. <u>Student</u> is to <u>pupil</u> as <u>bad</u> is to <u>wicked</u>. (same meanings)
3. <u>Billy</u> is to <u>nickname</u> as <u>hammer</u> is to <u>tool</u>. (examples)

Did you notice?

The first and second sets in each sentence have the same kinds of pairs.

Do you remember?

Two sets put together must have the same kinds of pairs.

Try it out.

Here is a word list.
Choose the word that **best** fits the blank.
Not all the words fit.
A word may be used only once.

WORD LIST

anxious	calm	guest	large	love
normal	pain	tiny	unusual	value

1. Positive is to sure as appreciate is to _____.

2. Gentle is to rough as peculiar is to _____ .

3. Conceal is to hide as visitor is to _____ .

4. Fortune is to luck as distress is to _____ .

5. Thief is to crook as worried is to _____ .

STOP   CHECK ANSWERS ON PAGE 118.

LESSON 6

Match each word with its meaning.

____	**1.** excited	**a.** to talk very softly
____	**2.** positive	**b.** worth a lot
____	**3.** conceal	**c.** having strong feelings
____	**4.** valuable	**d.** sure
____	**5.** whisper	**e.** to hide

LESSON 7

Match each word with its meaning.

____	**1.** anxious	**a.** promise
____	**2.** appreciate	**b.** more
____	**3.** additional	**c.** gentle
____	**4.** guarantee	**d.** worried
____	**5.** mild	**e.** to feel grateful

LESSON 8

Match each word with its meaning.

____	**1.** advice	**a.** luck
____	**2.** bakery	**b.** a person visiting someone's home
____	**3.** fortune	**c.** different kinds of things
____	**4.** guest	**d.** what someone says you should do
____	**5.** variety	**e.** a place where bread is made and sold

GO ON TO THE NEXT PAGE.

LESSON 9

Match each word with its meaning.

_____ 1. apartment

_____ 2. dependable

_____ 3. perfect

_____ 4. peculiar

_____ 5. surprise

a. something that someone doesn't expect

b. strange

c. a set of rooms in a building in which people live

d. the best something can be

e. able to be counted on

LESSON 10

Match each word with its meaning.

_____ 1. disguise

_____ 2. extraordinary

_____ 3. thief

_____ 4. fragile

_____ 5. distress

a. very delicate

b. to cause sadness

c. to try to look like someone else

d. very unusual

e. crook

STOP CHECK ANSWERS ON PAGE 118.

66

Count how many items you answered correctly in each review lesson. Write your score for each review lesson in the My Scores column. If all your scores are as high as the Good Scores, go on to Unit Three. If any of your review lesson scores are lower than the Good Scores, study the Review Pages. Then go on to Unit Three.

Lesson	Good Scores	My Scores	Review Pages
6	4 or 5		36–40
7	4 or 5		41–45
8	4 or 5		46–50
9	4 or 5		51–55
10	4 or 5		56–60

SENTENCE CLUES: OPPOSITES (ANTONYMS)

Read the following:

What is the meaning of <u>lean</u>?

1. Jean will eat lean meat only.
2. Her brother, however, likes fatty meat.

Did you notice?

Sentence 2 has two clues.
<u>However</u> tells you an opposite may follow.
Therefore, you know that <u>fatty</u> is the opposite of <u>lean</u>.
<u>Lean</u> means "without fat."

Try it out.

Words from this lesson are in sentences.
There is a line under these words.
Use sentence clues to figure out word meanings.
Write the meaning of each underlined word.

1. My family has changed its diet. We now eat more <u>lean</u> meat. We do not eat fatty meat.

_____

2. My family's eating habits are now good. They used to be <u>dreadful</u>.

_____

3. We used to put lots of sugar in our food. We liked everything to taste sweet. We did not like anything to taste <u>bitter</u>.

_____

4. However, now we use less sugar. We have tried to <u>reduce</u> the amount of sugar we eat.

_____

GO ON TO THE NEXT PAGE.

5. It was <u>important</u> to change our diet. We felt that change was very much needed. Now we all feel better.

STOP CHECK ANSWERS ON PAGE 118.

WORDS AND THEIR MEANINGS

Here are the words in this lesson.
Learn the meanings of the words.

1. **bitter** (bit′ ur) (Describing word)   Not sweet.
   I do not like anything that tastes <u>bitter</u>.
2. **dreadful** (dred′ ful) (Describing word)   Awful; terrible.
   There was a <u>dreadful</u> fire. Many people were hurt.
3. **important** (im · por′ tint) (Describing word)   Valuable; of great worth; very much needed.
   Water is <u>important</u> to life.
4. **lean** (lēn) (Describing word)   Not fat; slender; thin.
   Please buy <u>lean</u> meat for me. (not fat)
   She is very <u>lean</u>. (slender)
5. **reduce** (ri · dōōs′) (Action word)   To make less or smaller; to lower; to decrease.
   <u>Reduce</u> the heat under the pot. Otherwise, the food will burn.

Try it out.

Below are meanings for each word in this lesson.
Choose the word from the word list that fits the meaning.

WORD LIST

bitter   dreadful   important   lean   reduce

1. To lower _____

2. Very much needed _____

3. Slender _____

4. Terrible _____

5. Not sweet _____

STOP   CHECK ANSWERS ON PAGE 118.

71

Read the following:

1. I love cookies and cake.	1. I love cookies and cake.
2. I also like fruits.	2. I also like fruits.
3. I do not like bitter food.	3. I do not like sweet food.

Did you notice?

The word <u>sweet</u> does not fit in sentence 3.
The word <u>bitter</u> fits in sentence 3.
The other sentences help you figure out what word fits.

Try it out.

Fill in each blank. Choose the **best** word for each blank.

1. My doctor wants me to eat ＿＿＿＿＿＿＿ food only. He wants me to lose weight. (fatty or lean)

2. I am going to eat less. I really want to ＿＿＿＿＿＿＿ my weight. (increase or reduce)

3. The doctor said I could have a heart attack. That frightened me. That would be ＿＿＿＿＿＿＿. (fortunate or dreadful)

4. Changing my diet is ＿＿＿＿＿＿＿. I need to eat better. I also need to walk more. (difficult or important)

5. I like lemons. I like their ＿＿＿＿＿＿＿ taste. Fortunately, they are not bad for me. (sweet or bitter)

STOP CHECK ANSWERS ON PAGE 119.

Word opposites are called antonyms.
Antonyms are good word clues.
They can help you figure out word meanings.

Try it out.

Here is a story.
It has missing words.
Here is a word list.
Fill in each blank with a word from the word list.
A word may be used only once.

WORD LIST

bitter   dreadful   important   lean   reduce

I've always wanted to be _____ . I'm not really fat. Still, I'd
                              (1)

look better if I could _____ my weight. The problem is I can't
                           (2)

stand things that taste _____ . I love sweets. I feel they are
                            (3)

_____ to my life. I can't live without them. Don't you agree?
       (4)

Wouldn't life be _____ without dessert? The joy would be gone.
                      (5)

Read the following:

What is the meaning of <u>gift</u>?

1. It is Sharon's birthday.
2. We are having a party.
3. Everyone is bringing a gift.
4. I bought her an expensive present.

Did you notice?

The sentences give you clues to the meaning of <u>gift</u>.
The sentences explain why you are giving a present.
You give a <u>gift</u> because it is someone's birthday.
The clue in sentence 4 is <u>present</u>.
<u>Gift</u> and <u>present</u> have the same meaning.

Do you remember?

Writers often use more than one kind of sentence clue.

Try it out.

Words from this lesson are in sentences.
There is a line under these words.
Use sentence clues to figure out word meanings.
Write the meaning of each underlined word.

1. What is the <u>amount</u> of money you owe? Do you have enough?

---

2. What kind of <u>gift</u> are you buying? I don't know what present to buy.

---

3. Please <u>reserve</u> a table for us at the restaurant. Please save us a table by the window.

GO ON TO THE NEXT PAGE.

4. Will you be able to <u>mend</u> this dress? I don't know how to fix it.

_____

5. Her <u>natural</u> hair color is brown. She colored it blond.

_____

STOP CHECK ANSWERS ON PAGE 119.

Here are the words in this lesson.
Learn the meanings of the words.

1. **amount** (uh · mount') (Naming word) Quantity; how much someone has; the total.
   I don't have the right <u>amount</u> of change. Can you lend me a dime?

2. **gift** (gift) (Naming word) Present; something given to someone else.
   Thank you so much for the lovely birthday <u>gift</u>.

3. **mend** (mend) (Action word) To repair; to fix.
   I need someone to <u>mend</u> my fence. It is broken.

4. **natural** (natch' ur · ul) (Describing word) Normal; not fake; real; being born with.
   It is <u>natural</u> to want what is best for your family. (normal)
   My <u>natural</u> hair color is red. (real)
   He is a <u>natural</u> ball player. (being born with)

5. **reserve** (ri · zurv') (Action word) To save; to put away for another time; to store; to hold back; to set aside.
   I <u>reserved</u> two theater seats. They are saving the seats for me.

Try it out.

Below are meanings for each word in this lesson.
Choose the word from the word list that fits the meaning.

WORD LIST

amount   gift   mend   natural   reserve

1. Present _____

2. Normal _____

3. Quantity _____

4. Save _____

5. Repair _____

STOP CHECK ANSWERS ON PAGE 119.

Read the following:

1. Hank spends all his money.
2. He never saves any.
3. By Friday, he has none left.
4. He'll have to learn to reserve some money for the end of the week.

1. Hank spends all his money.
2. He never saves any.
3. By Friday, he has none left.
4. He'll have to learn to reduce some money for the end of the week.

Did you notice?

The word <u>reduce</u> does not fit in sentence 4.
The word <u>reserve</u> fits in sentence 4.
The other sentences help you figure out what word fits.

Try it out.

Fill in each blank. Choose the **best** word for each blank.

1. Please try to act _____. I know it's hard to act normal at a time like this. (fair or natural)

2. What _____ do we need? Let's buy only one pound. (present or amount)

3. Please _____ my pants. I ripped them at work. (rush or mend)

4. What _____ are you getting her for her birthday? (amount or gift)

5. I will _____ a room for you at the hotel. (decrease or reserve)

STOP CHECK ANSWERS ON PAGE 119.

SENTENCE CLUES: WORDS WITH THE SAME MEANING (SYNONYMS)

12

> Words with the same meaning are called synonyms.
> Synonyms are good word clues.
> They can help you figure out word meanings.

Try it out.

Here is a story.
It has missing words.
Here is a word list.
Fill in each blank with a word from the word list.
A word may be used only once.

WORD LIST

amount   gifts   mend   natural   reserves

My mother works in a tailor shop. Her job is to _____ (1)

dresses. She works part-time. The _____ (2) of money she earns is

not a lot. However, it helps. She _____ (3) the money to buy

additional things. For example, she will buy each of us _____ (4)

for our birthday. It makes her feel good to do this. She feels it's

_____ (5) to want to make your children happy.

STOP CHECK ANSWERS ON PAGE 119.

78

Read the following:

What is the meaning of <u>disease</u>?

1. Doctors have patients with different diseases.
2. Children usually have diseases such as the mumps or measles.
3. Adults usually have other kinds of diseases.

Did you notice?

The mumps and measles are examples of diseases.
They help you figure out the meaning of disease.
<u>Disease</u> means "illness" or "sickness."

Do you remember?

Examples are not the meaning of a word.
An example is one thing that stands for others.
Examples help you figure out word meanings.

Try it out.

Words from this lesson are in sentences.
There is a line under these words.
Use sentence clues to figure out word meanings.
Write the meaning of each underlined word.

1. My friend and I work in different places. Joe works in a shoe <u>factory</u>.

   He makes sneakers. I help make cars. I work in an auto <u>factory</u>.

---

2. Last year I got chicken pox. This <u>disease</u> is usually a children's disease.

---

3. My friends thought it was funny. However, getting chicken pox as an

   adult can be <u>serious</u>. It can be dangerous.

GO ON TO THE NEXT PAGE.

4. I was very uncomfortable. I kept sending my mother on <u>errands</u>. She went to the store five times for me. She got my medicine. She bought me magazines. I kept her busy.

---

5. I had little bumps all over. I <u>itched</u> all over. I wanted to scratch my whole body. However, I couldn't. Scratching would make me worse.

STOP CHECK ANSWERS ON PAGE 119.

Here are the words in this lesson.
Learn the meanings of the words.

1. **disease** (di · zēz′) (Naming word)   Illness; sickness.
   The doctors didn't know what <u>disease</u> he had.
2. **errand** (er′ ind) (Naming word)   A short trip to do something,
   sometimes for someone else.
   My mother sent me on an <u>errand</u> to buy her a newspaper.
3. **factory** (fak′ tuh · rē) (Naming word)   A place where things are
   made by hand or machine.
   My father and brother work in a radio <u>factory</u>.
4. **itch** (itch) (Naming word)   An uncomfortable feeling that makes
   you want to scratch your skin. (Action word)   To feel like
   scratching.
   I have an <u>itch</u>. I was stung by a bee.
5. **serious** (sir′ ē · us) (Describing word)   Not funny or joking;
   needing a lot of thinking; dangerous or cause for worry; important.
   The bee sting could be <u>serious</u>.   (dangerous)
   He spoke about something very <u>serious</u>.   (important)
   Let's give that some <u>serious</u> thought.   (needing a lot of thinking)

Try it out.

Below are meanings for each word in this lesson.
Choose the word from the word list that fits the meaning.

WORD LIST
disease   errand   factory   itch   serious

1. A short trip to do something, usually for someone else _____

2. Illness _____

3. An uncomfortable feeling that makes you want to scratch _____

4. Needing a lot of thinking _____

5. A place where things are made by hand or machine _____

STOP CHECK ANSWERS ON PAGE 119.

Read the following:

1. My daughter has the mumps.
2. My son has the measles.
3. My husband has the flu.
4. Everyone in my family has a different disease.

1. My daughter has the mumps.
2. My son has the measles.
3. My husband has the flu.
4. Everyone in my family has a different cold.

Did you notice?

The word <u>cold</u> does not fit in sentence 4.
The word <u>disease</u> fits in sentence 4.
The other sentences help you figure out what word fits.

Try it out.

Fill in each blank. Choose the **best** word for each blank.

1. Please don't laugh about this. It is _____. (ordinary or serious)

2. My skin is raw from scratching. I've had an _____ all day. (errand or itch)

3. My son has never had any _____. He has never even had a cold. (disease or itch)

4. I need to go on one more _____. I forgot to buy milk. (vacation or errand)

5. We make dresses in this _____. It's a large building. There are three hundred people working here. (apartment or factory)

STOP CHECK ANSWERS ON PAGE 119.

An example is one thing that stands for others.
Examples are good word clues.
They can help you figure out word meanings.

Try it out.
Here is a story.
It has missing words.
Here is a word list.
Fill in each blank with a word from the word list.
A word may be used only once.

WORD LIST

disease   errands   factory   itch   serious

My brother and I work in a(n) _____. We make seat belts
                                   (1)
for cars. Last week, some workers became ill. First they got a rash. Soon

they began to _____. Then they had a high fever. They had
                    (2)
to be taken to the hospital. The doctors said they had an unusual

_____. However, they said it was not _____. The
      (3)   (4)
doctors could treat it. The workers would have to stay in the hospital for a

few days. We told them we would do their _____ for them. We
                                                (5)
would buy anything they needed. We helped them out until they got better.

STOP CHECK ANSWERS ON PAGE 119.

Read the following:

What is the meaning of <u>introduce</u>?

1. Luis said he would introduce me to many people.
2. At the party, I met his brother.
3. Then I met his girlfriend.
4. I shook hands with everyone Luis presented me to.
5. I got to know lots of people.

Did you notice?

Sentences 2 through 5 give you sentence clues.
They help you figure out the meaning of <u>introduce</u>.
Sentences 2 and 3 are examples of people Luis met.
Sentences 4 and 5 describe the word introduce.
<u>Introduce</u> means "to present one person to another."

Do you remember?

Pictures in words are descriptions.
Descriptions do not give word meanings.
They help you figure out word meanings.

Try it out.

Words from this lesson are in sentences.
There is a line under these words.
Use sentence clues to figure out word meanings.
Write the meaning of each underlined word.

1. Alanda does not like me to <u>introduce</u> her to anyone. Last night I wanted her to meet some people. She did not want to meet them. She has a difficult time getting to know new people.

GO ON TO THE NEXT PAGE.

2. I love to meet new people. I work as a <u>receptionist</u>. My job is to meet people at the office.

___

3. I <u>greet</u> the people who come to our office. I smile at them and say, "Hello."

___

4. I ask them their names. Then I ask whom they want to see. My <u>objective</u> is to make them comfortable. My purpose is to help them feel at home.

___

5. I work in a <u>magnificent</u> office. It has thick blue carpeting and fancy furniture. It is very large and beautiful.

___

STOP CHECK ANSWERS ON PAGE 119.

Here are the words in this lesson.
Learn the meanings of the words.

1. **greet** (grēt) (Action word) To welcome or meet in a friendly way; to give good wishes to someone you meet.
John always says "Good morning" to me. I <u>greet</u> him nicely, too.

2. **introduce** (in · truh · dōōs′) (Action word) To present one person to another; to bring in or add something new.
At the party, I <u>introduced</u> my guests to my boyfriend. (to present)
Computers have <u>introduced</u> us to a new vocabulary. (to add something new)

3. **magnificent** (mag · nif′ i · sunt) (Describing word) Very beautiful; grand; extraordinary; rich; wonderful.
Mrs. Johnson's home is <u>magnificent</u>. It is very large and grandly decorated.

4. **objective** (ob · jek′ tiv) (Naming word) Goal; aim; what you want at the end.
My <u>objective</u> in life is to be happy.

5. **receptionist** (ri · sep′ shun · ist) (Naming word) A person whose job is to welcome visitors to an office.
The <u>receptionist</u> told us to be seated. She said that Mrs. Smith would see us soon.

Try it out.

Below are meanings for each word in this lesson.
Choose the word from the word list that fits the meaning.

WORD LIST

greet   introduce   magnificent   objective   receptionist

1. Goal _____

2. To give good wishes to someone _____

GO ON TO THE NEXT PAGE.

3. Very grand and beautiful _____

4. To bring in something new _____

5. A person whose job is to welcome visitors _____

STOP CHECK ANSWERS ON PAGE 119.

Read the following:

1. This apartment is large.	1. This apartment is large.
2. It has high ceilings.	2. It has high ceilings.
3. It has big windows.	3. It has big windows.
4. The rooms are beautiful.	4. The rooms are beautiful.
5. The apartment is magnificent.	5. The apartment is ugly.

Did you notice?

The word <u>ugly</u> does not fit in sentence 5.
The word <u>magnificent</u> fits in sentence 5.
The other sentences help you figure out what word fits.

Try it out.

Fill in each blank. Choose the **best** word for each blank.

1. Sally likes to meet people. Her job as a _____ is perfect for her. (customer or receptionist)

2. Sally likes to _____ people. She always smiles and says, "Hello." (surprise or greet)

3. Her _____ is to make them feel comfortable. (advice or objective)

4. Sally often has to _____ people to one another. For example, she says, "Ms. Smith, I'd like you to meet Mr. Brown." (greet or introduce)

5. Sally's office is large. The carpeting is blue. The furniture is fancy. It is _____. (objective or magnificent)

STOP CHECK ANSWERS ON PAGE 120.

A picture in words is a description.
A description is a sentence clue.
It can help you figure out word meanings.

Try it out.

Here is a story.
It has missing words.
Here is a word list.
Fill in each blank with a word from the word list.
A word may be used only once.

WORD LIST

greet   introduce   magnificent   objective   receptionist

I am very fortunate. I work in a(n) _____ office. It is large
                                         (1)

and beautiful. I have my own business. My wife works with me. She is the

_____ . She knows how to _____ people. She knows
      (2)   (3)

how to make them feel comfortable. She is always friendly. She is always

trying to get people to meet one another. She loves to _____
                                                              (4)

young people to one another. Her _____ is to get young men and
                                        (5)

women together. She is very good at doing this. We have already been

invited to three weddings.

STOP   CHECK ANSWERS ON PAGE 120.

Read the following:

What is the meaning of jealous?

1. Ben was jealous.
2. His girlfriend was going out with another man.

Did you notice?

Sentence 2 tells why Ben is jealous.
The reason helps you figure out the meaning of jealous.
Jealous means "being angry when someone you love sees someone else."

Do you remember?

The reason for something is an explanation.
An explanation is a good sentence clue.

Try it out.

Words from this lesson are in sentences.
There is a line under these words.
Use sentence clues to figure out word meanings.
Write the meaning of each underlined word.

1. Vera was very jealous. Her boyfriend said he was going out with

   someone else. He didn't love her anymore.

---

2. Vera started to cry. She went for a ride in her car. Her eyes were filled

   with tears. A car pulled out in front of her. She couldn't stop. She had

   an accident. She crashed into the car.

GO ON TO THE NEXT PAGE.

3. The crash killed the person in the other car. The person in the car was the new girlfriend. Some people said Vera <u>murdered</u> her.

---

4. They called it a <u>crime</u>. They said Vera drove her car into the other. However, Vera said she had not done anything wrong. She had not done anything against the law.

---

5. She said she was not <u>guilty</u>. She should not be blamed. She did not want it to happen. She could have gotten killed.

STOP CHECK ANSWERS ON PAGE 120.

Here are the words in this lesson.
Learn the meanings of the words.

1. **accident** (ak′ si · dent) (Naming word) Something that takes place that is not expected; something that happens by chance; something bad or harmful that takes place that is not expected.
There was a terrible car <u>accident</u>. Ten people got hurt.

2. **crime** (krīm) (Naming word) Something done that is against the law.
He robbed a bank. He went to jail for this <u>crime</u>.

3. **guilty** (gil′ tē) (Describing word) Feeling bad about having done something wrong; having broken the law; deserving blame.
The man said he wasn't <u>guilty</u>. He said he didn't rob the store. (deserving blame)
The woman felt <u>guilty</u> about not telling about the accident. (feeling bad about having done something wrong)

4. **jealous** (jel′ us) (Describing word) Being angry when someone you like or love sees someone else; being angry when another has something or someone you feel is yours.
Mary is <u>jealous</u> when her boyfriend even talks to another woman.

5. **murder** (mur′ dur) (Naming word) A killing of one person by another. (Action word) To kill.
The police said it was <u>murder</u>. Someone had killed her.

Try it out.

Below are meanings for each word in this lesson.
Choose the word from the word list that fits the meaning.

WORD LIST
accident   crime   guilty   jealous   murder

1. To kill someone _____

2. Being angry when someone you like sees someone else _____

GO ON TO THE NEXT PAGE.

3. Something that takes place that is not expected _____

4. Something that is done that is against the law _____

5. Feeling bad about having done something wrong _____

STOP CHECK ANSWERS ON PAGE 120.

Read the following:

1. Mr. Wang owns a gun.	1. Mr. Wang owns a gun.
2. His child was playing with it.	2. His child was playing with it.
3. It went off by mistake.	3. It went off by mistake.
4. The child was shot.	4. The child was shot.
5. It was an accident.	5. It was planned.

Did you notice?

The word <u>planned</u> does not fit in sentence 5.
The word <u>accident</u> fits in sentence 5.
The other sentences help you figure out what word fits.

Try it out.

Fill in each blank. Choose the **best** word for each blank.

1. Lisa doesn't like her boyfriend to look at other girls. She is

   _____. (guilty or jealous)

2. The robber was found to be _____. He had to go to jail.

   (jealous or guilty)

3. Yesterday I had a dreadful _____. I fell down the stairs and

   broke my leg. (crime or accident)

4. Drunk driving is a(n) _____. You can go to jail for doing

   that. (crime or accident)

5. _____ is a dreadful problem in the city. More and more

   people are being killed. (Accident or Murder)

STOP CHECK ANSWERS ON PAGE 120.

SENTENCE CLUES: THE REASON FOR SOMETHING (EXPLANATION)

> The reason for something is an explanation.
> An explanation is a good sentence clue.
> It can help you figure out word meanings.

Try it out.

Here is a story.
It has missing words.
Here is a word list.
Fill in each blank with a word from the word list.
A word may be used only once.

WORD LIST

accident   crime   guilty   jealous   murder

Paul was cleaning his gun. It went off by _____. His friend
(1)

was shot. The police said he tried to _____ his friend. The police
(2)

said it wasn't a mistake. They said Paul was _____ because his
(3)

friend was going out with Paul's girlfriend. Paul said it wasn't

true. He wasn't _____. He didn't want his friend to get hurt. He
(4)

said it wasn't a(n) _____ to have a gun. However, the police said
(5)

he should have been more careful. People who own guns must be very

careful. They cannot point them at people. They must know how to

clean them.

STOP CHECK ANSWERS ON PAGE 120.

EXTRA WORD POWER

Y. Full of.

Y is found at the end of many words. **Y** at the end of a word means "full of." **Y** often makes a naming word (noun) a describing word (adjective).

Examples with y: dirty—full of dirt; itchy—full of itches; sleepy—full of sleep; muddy—full of mud; rusty—full of rust; sandy—full of sand.

How many more **y** words can you think of?

WORDS IN SENTENCES (LESSONS 11–15)

Here are sentences using some of the words in this unit.
Examples:

1. (receptionist; errand)
   The receptionist went on an errand for her boss.
2. (serious; disease)
   Maria had a serious disease.

Try it out.

Write a sentence with the words given below.

1. (guilty; crime)

_____

2. (dreadful; accident)

_____

3. (receptionist; greets)

_____

4. (magnificent; gift)

_____

5. (important; mend)

_____

STOP CHECK SAMPLE SENTENCES ON PAGE 120.

WORD PAIRS THAT GO TOGETHER (ANALOGIES)

Read the following:

1. <u>Lean</u> is to <u>fat</u> as <u>decrease</u> is to <u>increase</u>.   (opposites)
2. <u>Bashful</u> is to <u>shy</u> as <u>guarantee</u> is to <u>promise</u>.   (same meanings)
3. <u>Giant</u> is to <u>gigantic</u> as <u>fly</u> is to <u>tiny</u>.   (examples)

Did you notice?

The first and second sets in each sentence have the same kinds of pairs.

Do you remember?

Two sets put together must have the same kinds of pairs.

Try it out.

Here is a word list.
Choose the word that **best** fits the blank.
Not all the words fit.
A word may be used only once.

WORD LIST

break	disease	flower	goal	murder
present	problem	repair	slender	thief

1. Hammer is to tool as mumps is to _____.

2. Clumsy is to awkward as gift is to _____.

3. Ordinary is to unusual as mend is to _____.

4. Month is to January as crime is to _____.

5. Comfortable is to restful as objective is to _____.

STOP CHECK ANSWERS ON PAGE 120.

WORD PAIRS THAT GO TOGETHER (ANALOGIES)

Read the following:

1. <u>Simple</u> is to <u>hard</u> as <u>mild</u> is to <u>harsh</u>.   (opposites)
2. <u>Anxious</u> is to <u>worried</u> as <u>positive</u> is to <u>sure</u>.   (same meanings)
3. <u>Candy</u> is to <u>sweet</u> as <u>lemon</u> is to <u>sour</u>.   (examples)

Did you notice?

The first and second sets in each sentence have the same kinds of pairs.

Do you remember?

Two sets put together must have the same kinds of pairs.

Try it out.

Here is a word list.
Choose the word that **best** fits the blank.
Not all the words fit.
A word may be used only once.

WORD LIST

awful   cold   crime   disease   fake
less   murder   normal   quantity   save

1. Disease is to illness as reserve is to _____.

2. Serious is to silly as natural is to _____.

3. Fall is to accident as robbery is to _____.

4. Mend is to fix as amount is to _____.

5. Magnificent is to grand as dreadful is to _____.

STOP CHECK ANSWERS ON PAGE 120.

LESSON 11

Match each word with its meaning.

____	1. bitter	**a.** decrease
____	2. lean	**b.** valuable
____	3. reduce	**c.** terrible
____	4. dreadful	**d.** not sweet
____	5. important	**e.** thin

LESSON 12

Match each word with its meaning.

____	1. reserve	**a.** quantity
____	2. amount	**b.** present
____	3. mend	**c.** save
____	4. natural	**d.** fix
____	5. gift	**e.** normal

LESSON 13

Match each word with its meaning.

____	1. disease	**a.** needing a lot of thinking
____	2. errand	**b.** to feel like scratching
____	3. factory	**c.** illness
____	4. itch	**d.** a short trip to do something
____	5. serious	**e.** a place where things are made

GO ON TO THE NEXT PAGE.

LESSON 14

Match each word with its meaning.

_____ **1.** greet

_____ **2.** introduce

_____ **3.** magnificent

_____ **4.** objective

_____ **5.** receptionist

a. grand

b. a person whose job is to welcome visitors

c. to give good wishes to a person you meet

d. to bring in something new

e. goal

LESSON 15

Match each word with its meaning.

_____ **1.** accident

_____ **2.** crime

_____ **3.** guilty

_____ **4.** jealous

_____ **5.** murder

a. being angry when someone you love sees someone else

b. something that takes place that is not expected

c. to kill

d. feeling bad about having done something wrong

e. something done that is against the law

STOP CHECK ANSWERS ON PAGES 120 AND 121.

Count how many items you answered correctly in each review lesson. Write your score for each review lesson in the My Scores column. If all your scores are as high as the Good Scores, take the Posttest on page 103. If any of your review lesson scores are lower than the Good Scores, study the review pages. Then take the Posttest.

Lesson	Good Scores	My Scores	Review Pages
11	4 or 5		69–73
12	4 or 5		74–78
13	4 or 5		79–83
14	4 or 5		84–89
15	4 or 5		90–95

LESSON 1

Write the meaning of each underlined word.

1. The <u>considerate</u> woman always gives cookies to the children.

_____

2. Is it <u>fair</u> for you to eat it all?

_____

3. Will you <u>decrease</u> the number of jobs here?

_____

4. This <u>sloppy</u> room needs to be cleaned.

_____

5. Can you <u>repair</u> the water leak?

_____

LESSON 2

Here are five words. Write the word that goes with the meaning.

WORD LIST

damp   glossy   guard   ordinary   wicked

1. A person who protects someone _____

2. Shiny _____

3. Evil _____

4. Moist _____

5. Normal _____

GO ON TO THE NEXT PAGE.

LESSON 3

Fill in each blank with a word from the word list. A word may be used only once.

WORD LIST

gigantic   grateful   intend   pity   visit

1. We would like you to _____ our home.

2. Some buildings in large cities are _____ .

3. We are _____ for your help.

4. Do you _____ to go to the party?

5. We felt _____ for the badly hurt man.

LESSON 4

Match each word with its meaning.

____ 1. strange   **a.** cozy

____ 2. awkward   **b.** to say one is unwilling to accept

____ 3. bashful   **c.** unusual

____ 4. refuse   **d.** clumsy

____ 5. comfortable   **e.** shy

LESSON 5

Fill in each blank with a word from the word list. A word may be used only once.

WORD LIST

advertisement   hopeful   part-time   rush   secretary

1. I work four hours a day at my _____ job.

2. Sara needs to _____ to catch the bus.

3. Her _____ answers all her mail.

4. Did the _____ help you get a job?

5. Jack is _____ that he will do well.

GO ON TO THE NEXT PAGE.

LESSON 6

Write the meaning of each underlined word.

1. That is a very <u>valuable</u> painting.

_____

2. Please <u>conceal</u> the present until her birthday.

_____

3. You should <u>whisper</u> in the library.

_____

4. We are <u>positive</u> you are wrong.

_____

5. The <u>excited</u> child jumped up and down.

_____

LESSON 7

Match each word with its meaning.

____ 1. appreciate   **a.** gentle

____ 2. anxious   **b.** promise

____ 3. additional   **c.** to feel grateful

____ 4. mild   **d.** extra

____ 5. guarantee   **e.** worried

LESSON 8

Here are five words. Write the word that goes with the meaning.

WORD LIST

advice   bakery   fortune   guest   variety

1. A person visiting another's house _____

2. What someone says you should do _____

GO ON TO THE NEXT PAGE.

3. A lot of money _____

4. Many different kinds of things _____

5. A place where cakes are made and sold _____

LESSON 9

Write the meaning of each underlined word.

1. Everything he does is always <u>perfect</u>.

_____

2. The <u>peculiar</u> man frightened us.

_____

3. The party was a <u>surprise</u>.

_____

4. I will only marry someone very <u>dependable</u>.

_____

5. Our <u>apartment</u> is sunny and large.

_____

LESSON 10

Fill in each blank with a word from the word list. A word may be used only once.

WORD LIST

disguise　　distress　　extraordinary　　fragile　　thief

1. That is the most _____ thing I have ever seen.

2. The _____ tried to rob us.

3. Our problems gave us a lot of _____ .

4. The _____ glass broke easily.

5. The crook wore a mask to _____ himself.

GO ON TO THE NEXT PAGE.

LESSON 11

Here are five words. Write the word that goes with the meaning.

WORD LIST

bitter   dreadful   important   lean   reduce

1. Awful _____

2. Valuable _____

3. Slender _____

4. Not sweet _____

5. To lower _____

LESSON 12

Fill in each blank with a word from the word list. A word may be used only once.

WORD LIST

amount   gift   mend   natural   reserve

1. Is this the right _____ of money?

2. We bought a nice _____ for your birthday.

3. I like _____ foods only.

4. We will _____ a table for you at the restaurant.

5. Can you _____ this tear?

LESSON 13

Write the meaning of each underlined word.

1. I work in a very large <u>factory</u>.

_____

2. I need to go on an <u>errand</u> for my wife.

_____

3. This <u>itch</u> is driving me crazy.

_____

GO ON TO THE NEXT PAGE.

4. Fortunately, they do not have any <u>disease</u>.

_____

5. This illness can be <u>serious</u>.

_____

LESSON 14

Fill in each blank with a word from the word list. A word may be used only once.

WORD LIST

greet   introduce   magnificent   objective   receptionist

1. Our _____ is to win.

2. The _____ is a friendly person.

3. The _____ picture took our breath away.

4. Please _____ that handsome man to me.

5. How should I _____ him?

LESSON 15

Write the meaning of each underlined word.

1. Is she really <u>guilty</u> of stealing?

_____

2. How could anyone <u>murder</u> a child?

_____

3. He was <u>jealous</u> of his wife's men friends.

_____

4. Murder is a terrible <u>crime</u>.

_____

5. Are you sure it wasn't an <u>accident</u>?

_____

STOP CHECK ANSWERS BEGINNING ON PAGE 121.

Count how many items you answered correctly in each lesson of the Posttest. Write your score for each lesson in the My Scores column. If all your Posttest lesson scores are as high as the Good Scores, go on to *Power Vocabulary 4,* Lesson 1. If any of your Posttest lesson scores are lower than the Good Scores, study the lessons on the assigned Review Pages again. Then go on to *Power Vocabulary 4,* Lesson 1.

Lesson	Good Scores	My Scores	Review Pages
1	All correct		2–6
2	All correct		7–11
3	All correct		12–16
4	All correct		17–21
5	All correct		22–27
6	All correct		36–40
7	All correct		41–45
8	All correct		46–50
9	All correct		51–55
10	All correct		56–60
11	All correct		69–73
12	All correct		74–78
13	All correct		79–83
14	All correct		84–89
15	All correct		90–95

The number after the meaning gives you the lesson the word is in.

Accident.   Something that takes place that is not expected; something that happens by chance; something bad or harmful that takes place that is not expected.   15

Additional.   More; extra.   7

Advertisement.   A notice of things for sale in a newspaper, on the radio, or on television; a list of jobs in a newspaper.   5

Advice.   What you tell people you think they should do; what someone says you should do.   8

Awkward.   Clumsy; not doing things smoothly; not handy.   4

Amount.   Quantity; how much someone has; the total.   12

Anxious.   Worried; uneasy.   7

Apartment.   A room or set of rooms in a building in which people live.   9

Appreciate.   To feel grateful; to value; to be thankful.   7

Bakery.   A place where bread, cookies, and cakes are made and sold.   8

Bashful.   Shy; timid.   4

Bitter.   Not sweet.   11

Comfortable.   Restful; cozy; free from worry.   4

Conceal.   To hide; to keep secret; to place out of sight.   6

Considerate.   Thoughtful of the feelings of others; caring of others; unselfish; helpful; nice; kind.   1

Crime.   Something done that is against the law.   15

Damp.   Wet; moist.   2

Decrease.   A becoming or making less or smaller; to become or make less or smaller.   1

Dependable. Able to be sure of; able to be counted on; always doing what one should.   9

Disease. Illness; sickness.   13

Disguise. Something that makes someone or something look like someone or something else; clothes or mask that hide who a person is; to hide who one is by wearing certain clothing or a mask; to try to look like someone or something else.   10

Distress. Pain; upset; to cause sadness or pain; to upset.   10

Dreadful. Awful; terrible.   11

Errand. A short trip to do something, sometimes for someone else.   13

Excited. Having or showing strong feelings; stirred up by feeling.   6

Extraordinary. Very unusual; great; going far beyond the ordinary.   10

Factory. A place where things are made by hand or machine.   13

Fair. Just; the way it should be; blond; light.   1

Fortune. A lot of money; riches; luck; what will happen to you.   8

Fragile. Very delicate; easily broken.   10

Gift. Present; something given to someone else.   12

Gigantic. Very large.   3

Glossy. Shiny.   2

Grateful. Thankful.   3

Greet. To welcome or meet in a friendly way; to give good wishes to someone you meet.   14

Guarantee. A promise; an agreement that something will be done or will work; to promise; to promise that something will be done or will work.   7

Guard. A person who protects someone or something; a person who watches over something or someone; to protect; to watch over.   2

Guest. A person visiting another's home or someplace.   8

Guilty.   Feeling bad about having done something wrong; having broken the law; deserving blame.   15

Hopeful.   Feeling that what you want to take place will take place; expecting to get what you want.   5

Important.   Valuable; of great worth; very much needed.   11

Intend.   To plan on doing something; to expect to do something.   3

Introduce.   To present one person to another; to bring or add something new.   14

Itch.   An uncomfortable feeling that makes you want to scratch your skin; to feel like scratching.   13

Jealous.   Being angry when someone you like or love sees someone else; being angry when another has something or someone you feel is yours.   15

Lean.   Not fat; slender; thin.   11

Magnificent.   Very beautiful; grand; extraordinary; rich; wonderful.   14

Mend.   To repair; to fix.   12

Mild.   Gentle; soft; not harsh; not strong.   7

Murder.   A killing of one person by another; to kill.   15

Natural.   Normal; not fake; real; being born with.   12

Objective.   Goal; aim; what you want at the end.   14

Ordinary.   Normal; usual; what you expect.   2

Part-time.   Working fewer hours than usual; working less than a full day; not working a full day.   5

Peculiar.   Not normal; unusual; out of the ordinary; strange; odd.   9

Perfect.   The best something can be; without anything wrong.   9

Pity.   A feeling sorry for; to feel sorry for.   3

Positive.   Sure; certain.   6

Receptionist.   A person whose job is to welcome visitors to an office.   14

Reduce.   To make less or smaller; to lower; to decrease.   11

Refuse.   To say or show one is unwilling to accept or do something.   4

Repair.   The act of fixing; to fix.   1

Reserve.   To save; to put away for another time; to store; to hold back; to set aside.   12

Rush.   The act of moving quickly or fast; the act of hurrying; to move quickly; to move fast; to hurry.   5

Secretary.   An office worker who answers the phone and letters for a boss.   5

Serious.   Not funny or joking; needing a lot of thinking; dangerous or cause for worry; important.   13

Sloppy.   Messy; not careful; careless; not neat.   1

Strange.   Not normal; unusual; not right; new.   4

Surprise.   Something that someone doesn't expect; to do something that someone doesn't expect.   9

Thief.   Robber; crook; a person who steals.   10

Valuable.   Costing a lot of money; worth a lot.   6

Variety.   Many different kinds of things.   8

Visit.   A short stay; a coming to see someone or something; to go to see someone or something.   3

Whisper.   Talking that is very soft; to talk very softly.   6

Wicked.   Bad; evil.   2

ANSWERS

LESSON 1
Word Meanings (p. 2)

1. fix
2. become less
3. just
4. messy
5. thoughtful of others

Word Meanings (List) (p. 4)

1. sloppy
2. fair
3. decrease
4. considerate
5. repair

Fill in the Blank (Choice) (p. 5)

1. increase
2. considerate
3. repair
4. sloppy
5. fair

Fill in the Blank (Story) (p. 6)

1. considerate
2. decrease
3. fair
4. sloppy
5. repairs

LESSON 2
Word Meanings (p. 7)

1. protects
2. normal
3. moist
4. evil
5. shiny

Word Meanings (List) (p. 9)

1. wicked
2. guard
3. ordinary
4. glossy
5. damp

Fill in the Blank (Choice) (p. 10)

1. ordinary
2. guard
3. wicked
4. damp
5. glossy

Fill in the Blank (Story) (p. 11)

1. ordinary
2. glossy
3. wicked
4. guard
5. damp

LESSON 3
Word Meanings (p. 12)

1. go to see
2. very large
3. planned
4. felt sorry for
5. thankful

Word Meanings (List) (p. 14)

1. pity
2. gigantic
3. visit
4. grateful
5. intend

Fill in the Blank (Choice) (p. 15)

1. intend
2. pity
3. visit
4. grateful
5. gigantic

Fill in the Blank (Story) (p. 16)

1. gigantic
2. visit
3. intend
4. grateful
5. pity

LESSON 4
Word Meanings (p. 17)

1. clumsy
2. is unwilling
3. shy
4. unusual
5. free from worry

Word Meanings (List) (p. 19)

1. strange
2. bashful
3. refuse
4. awkward
5. comfortable

Fill in the Blank (Choice) (p. 20)

1. friendly
2. strange
3. comfortable
4. refuse
5. awkward

Fill in the Blank (Story) (p. 21)

1. awkward
2. refuse
3. comfortable
4. bashful
5. strange

LESSON 5
Word Meanings (p. 22)

1. not working a full day
2. listings in the paper
3. an office worker who answers the phone and letters for a boss
4. hurried
5. expecting to get what you want

Word Meanings (List) (p. 24)

1. part-time
2. secretary
3. hopeful
4. advertisement
5. rush

Fill in the Blank (Choice) (p. 26)

1. hopeful
2. part-time
3. advertisement
4. rush
5. secretary

Fill in the Blank (Story) (p. 27)

1. secretary
2. advertisement
3. hopeful
4. part-time
5. rush

LESSONS 1–5
Words in Sentences (Sample Sentences) (p. 29)

1. It is considerate of you to visit me.
2. The guard will refuse to let you in.
3. It is a pity that she is so awkward.
4. The secretary did sloppy work.
5. I am very grateful you helped me repair my bike.

Word Pairs That Go Together (Analogies) (p. 30)

1. usual
2. increase
3. restful
4. just
5. gigantic

Word Pairs That Go Together (Analogies) (p. 31)

1. timid
2. thankful
3. wicked
4. guard
5. awkward

115

UNIT ONE REVIEW
Lesson 1 (p. 32)

1. c. to make smaller
2. e. just
3. d. caring of others
4. a. fix
5. b. messy

Lesson 2 (p. 32)

1. e. moist
2. d. shiny
3. b. to protect
4. a. usual
5. c. evil

Lesson 3 (p. 32)

1. d. very large
2. a. thankful
3. e. to feel sorry for
4. c. to plan on doing something
5. b. to go to see someone

Lesson 4 (p. 33)

1. b. shy
2. e. clumsy
3. d. cozy
4. a. unusual
5. c. to say one is unwilling to accept

Lesson 5 (p. 33)

1. c. a list of things for sale in a newspaper or on radio or TV
2. d. expecting to get what you want
3. a. working fewer hours than usual
4. e. to move fast
5. b. an office worker who answers the phone and letters for a boss

Lesson 6
Word Meanings (p. 36)

1. worth a lot
2. stirred up
3. speak softly
4. sure
5. hide

Word Meanings (List) (p. 38)

1. conceal
2. whisper
3. excited
4. valuable
5. positive

Fill in the Blank (Choice) (p. 39)

1. valuable
2. conceal
3. excited
4. positive
5. whisper

Fill in the Blank (Story) (p. 40)

1. conceal
2. whisper
3. excited
4. valuable
5. positive

Lesson 7
Word Meanings (p. 41)

1. gentle
2. extra
3. worried
4. am thankful for
5. promise

Word Meanings (List) (p. 43)

1. mild
2. guarantee
3. appreciate
4. additional
5. anxious

Fill in the Blank (Choice) (p. 44)

1. appreciate
2. additional
3. guarantees
4. anxious
5. mild

Fill in the Blank (Story) (p. 45)

1. anxious
2. additional
3. mild
4. appreciate
5. guarantee

Lesson 8
Word Meanings (p. 46)

1. place where they bake bread and cake
2. a lot of money
3. different kinds
4. people who visit
5. what someone says you should do

Word Meanings (List) (p. 48)

1. variety
2. fortune
3. guest
4. bakery
5. advice

Fill in the Blank (Choice) (p. 49)

1. fortune
2. bakery
3. guest
4. variety
5. advice

Fill in the Blank (Story) (p. 50)

1. guest
2. bakery
3. fortune
4. variety
5. advice

Lesson 9
Word Meanings (p. 51)

1. strange
2. able to be counted on
3. rooms in a building where people live
4. the best it can be
5. do something one doesn't expect

Word Meanings (List) (p. 53)

1. peculiar
2. surprise
3. dependable
4. apartment
5. perfect

Fill in the Blank (Choice) (p. 54)

1. dependable
2. apartment
3. perfect
4. peculiar
5. surprise

Fill in the Blank (Story) (p. 55)

1. peculiar
2. apartments
3. dependable
4. surprise
5. perfect

Lesson 10
Word Meanings (p. 56)

1. easily broken
2. robber
3. upset
4. very unusual
5. make things look different

Word Meanings (List) (p. 58)

1. thief
2. extraordinary
3. distress
4. fragile
5. disguise

Fill in the Blank (Choice) (p. 59)

1. disguise
2. fragile
3. extraordinary
4. distress
5. thief

Fill in the Blank (Story) (p. 60)

1. extraordinary
2. fragile
3. distress
4. thief
5. disguise

Lessons 6–10
Words in Sentences (Sample Sentences) (p. 62)

1. I buy a variety of doughnuts at the bakery.
2. A three bedroom apartment is perfect for my family.
3. She will be so excited when she sees the surprise I have for her.
4. I appreciate the good advice you gave me.
5. He wore such a peculiar disguise that we didn't know who he was.

Word Pairs That Go Together (Analogies) (p. 63)

1. promise
2. gentle
3. strong
4. apartment
5. unusual

Word Pairs That Go Together (Analogies) (p. 64)

1. value
2. normal
3. guest
4. pain
5. anxious

UNIT TWO REVIEW
Lesson 6 (p. 65)

1. c. having strong feelings
2. d. sure
3. e. to hide
4. b. worth a lot
5. a. to talk very softly

Lesson 7 (p. 65)

1. d. worried
2. e. to feel grateful
3. b. more
4. a. promise
5. c. gentle

Lesson 8 (p. 65)

1. d. what someone says you should do
2. e. a place where bread is made and sold
3. a. luck
4. b. a person visiting someone's home
5. c. different kinds of things

Lesson 9 (p. 66)

1. c. a set of rooms in a building in which people live
2. e. able to be counted on
3. d. the best something can be
4. b. strange
5. a. something that someone doesn't expect

Lesson 10 (p. 66)

1. c. to try to look like someone else
2. d. very unusual
3. e. crook
4. a. very delicate
5. b. to cause sadness

Lesson 11
Word Meanings (p. 69)

1. not fatty
2. awful
3. not sweet
4. lower
5. very much needed

Word Meanings (List) (p. 71)

1. reduce
2. important
3. lean
4. dreadful
5. bitter

Fill in the Blank (Choice) (p. 72)

1. lean
2. reduce
3. dreadful
4. important
5. bitter

Fill in the Blank (Story) (p. 73)

1. lean
2. reduce
3. bitter
4. important
5. dreadful

Lesson 12
Word Meanings (p. 74)

1. quantity
2. present
3. set aside or save
4. fix
5. real

Word Meanings (List) (p. 76)

1. gift
2. natural
3. amount
4. reserve
5. mend

Fill in the Blank (Choice) (p. 77)

1. natural
2. amount
3. mend
4. gift
5. reserve

Fill in the Blank (Story) (p. 78)

1. mend
2. amount
3. reserves
4. gifts
5. natural

Lesson 13
Word Meanings (p. 79)

1. a place where things are made
2. illness
3. dangerous or not funny
4. short trips to get things
5. felt like scratching

Word Meanings (List) (p. 81)

1. errand
2. disease
3. itch
4. serious
5. factory

Fill in the Blank (Choice) (p. 82)

1. serious
2. itch
3. disease
4. errand
5. factory

Fill in the Blank (Story) (p. 83)

1. factory
2. itch
3. disease
4. serious
5. errands

Lesson 14
Word Meanings (p. 84)

1. present one person to another
2. someone whose job is to welcome visitors to an office
3. welcome
4. aim
5. very beautiful and grand

Word Meanings (List) (p. 86)

1. objective
2. greet
3. magnificent
4. introduce
5. receptionist

Fill in the Blank (Choice) (p. 88)

1. receptionist
2. greet
3. objective
4. introduce
5. magnificent

Fill in the Blank (Story) (p. 89)

1. magnificent
2. receptionist
3. greet
4. introduce
5. objective

Lesson 15
Word Meanings (p. 90)

1. being angry when someone you like is seeing someone else
2. an unexpected happening
3. killed
4. something against the law
5. deserving blame

Word Meanings (List) (p. 92)

1. murder
2. jealous
3. accident
4. crime
5. guilty

Fill in the Blank (Choice) (p. 94)

1. jealous
2. guilty
3. accident
4. crime
5. Murder

Fill in the Blank (Story) (p. 95)

1. accident
2. murder
3. jealous
4. guilty
5. crime

Lessons 11–15
Words in Sentences (Sample Sentences) (p. 97)

1. He was guilty of the crime of murder.
2. Yesterday I had a dreadful accident.
3. My receptionist greets all my visitors.
4. I got a magnificent gift for my birthday.
5. It is important that I mend the roof today.

Word Pairs That Go Together (Analogies) (p. 98)

1. disease
2. present
3. break
4. murder
5. goal

Word Pairs That Go Together (Analogies) (p. 99)

1. save
2. fake
3. crime
4. quantity
5. awful

UNIT THREE REVIEW
Lesson 11 (p. 100)

1. **d.** not sweet
2. **e.** thin
3. **a.** decrease
4. **c.** terrible
5. **b.** valuable

Lesson 12 (p. 100)

1. **c.** save
2. **a.** quantity
3. **d.** fix
4. **e.** normal
5. **b.** present

Lesson 13 (p. 100)

1. **c.** illness
2. **d.** a short trip to do something
3. **e.** a place where things are made
4. **b.** to feel like scratching
5. **a.** needing a lot of thinking

Lesson 14 (p. 101)

1. **c.** to give good wishes to a person you meet
2. **d.** to bring in something new
3. **a.** grand
4. **e.** goal
5. **b.** a person whose job is to welcome visitors

Lesson 15 (p. 101)

1. **b.** something that takes place that is not expected
2. **e.** something done that is against the law
3. **d.** feeling bad about having done something wrong
4. **a.** being angry when someone you love sees someone else
5. **c.** to kill

Posttest (p. 103)
Lesson 1

1. caring of others
2. just
3. make less
4. messy
5. fix

Lesson 2

1. guard
2. glossy
3. wicked
4. damp
5. ordinary

Lesson 3

1. visit
2. gigantic
3. grateful
4. intend
5. pity

Lesson 4

1. **c.** unusual
2. **d.** clumsy
3. **e.** shy
4. **b.** to say one is unwilling to accept
5. **a.** cozy

Lesson 5

1. part-time
2. rush
3. secretary
4. advertisement
5. hopeful

Lesson 6

1. worth a lot
2. hide
3. talk very softly
4. sure
5. showing strong feelings

Lesson 7

1. **c.** to feel grateful
2. **e.** worried
3. **d.** extra
4. **a.** gentle
5. **b.** promise

Lesson 8

1. guest
2. advice
3. fortune
4. variety
5. bakery

Lesson 9

1. the best something can be
2. strange
3. something not expected
4. able to be counted on
5. set of rooms in a building people live in

Lesson 10

1. extraordinary
2. thief
3. distress
4. fragile
5. disguise

Lesson 11

1. dreadful
2. important
3. lean
4. bitter
5. reduce

Lesson 12

1. amount
2. gift
3. natural
4. reserve
5. mend

Lesson 13

1. a place where things are made by hand or machine
2. a short trip to do something
3. uncomfortable feeling that makes you want to scratch your skin
4. illness
5. dangerous

Lesson 14

1. objective
2. receptionist
3. magnificent
4. introduce
5. greet

Lesson 15

1. deserving blame
2. kill
3. being angry when someone you love sees someone else
4. something done that is against the law
5. something that takes place that is not expected